OPPOSING VIEWPOINTS® SERIES

Birth Control

Other Books of Related Interest:

Opposing Viewpoints Series

Parenting

Sexually Transmitted Diseases

Teen Dating

At Issue Series

Are Adoption Policies Fair?

Designer Babies

Sexting

Current Controversies Series

Health Care

Teen Pregnancy and Parenting

Teen Privacy

"Congress shall make no law ... abridging the freedom of speech, or of the press."

First Amendment to the US Constitution

The basic foundation of our democracy is the First Amendment guarantee of freedom of expression. The Opposing Viewpoints series is dedicated to the concept of this basic freedom and the idea that it is more important to practice it than to enshrine it.

OPPOSING VIEWPOINTS® SERIES

Birth Control

Margaret Haerens and Lynn M. Zott, Book Editors

GREENHAVEN PRESS
A part of Gale, Cengage Learning

GALE
CENGAGE Learning®

Detroit • New York • San Francisco • New Haven, Conn • Waterville, Maine • London

GALE
CENGAGE Learning·

Elizabeth Des Chenes, *Director, Publishing Solutions*

© 2012 Greenhaven Press, a part of Gale, Cengage Learning.

Gale and Greenhaven Press are registered trademarks used herein under license.

For more information, contact:
Greenhaven Press
27500 Drake Rd.
Farmington Hills, MI 48331-3535
Or you can visit our Internet site at gale.cengage.com

For product information and technology assistance, contact us at

Gale Customer Support, 1-800-877-4253
For permission to use material from this text or product, submit all requests online at www.cengage.com/permissions

Further permissions questions can be emailed to permissionrequest@cengage.com

Articles in Greenhaven Press anthologies are often edited for length to meet page requirements. In addition, original titles of these works are changed to clearly present the main thesis and to explicitly indicate the author's opinion. Every effort is made to ensure that Greenhaven Press accurately reflects the original intent of the authors. Every effort has been made to trace the owners of copyrighted material.

Cover Image copyright © Ocean/Corbis.

LIBRARY OF CONGRESS CATALOGING-IN-PUBLICATION DATA

Birth control / Margaret Haerens and Lynn M. Zott, book editors.
    p. cm. -- (Opposing viewpoints)
    Includes bibliographical references and index.
    ISBN 978-0-7377-6044-6 (hbk.) -- ISBN 978-0-7377-6045-3 (pbk.)
    1. Birth control. 2. Birth control--United States. I. Haerens, Margaret. II. Zott, Lynn M. (Lynn Marie), 1969-
    HQ766.B4793 2012
    613.9'43--dc23
                                                              2012005373

Printed in the United States of America
1 2 3 4 5 6 7 16 15 14 16 12

Contents

Chapter 4: What Is the Best Approach to Birth Control and Sex Education for Teens?

Why Consider
Opposing Viewpoints?

> *"The only way in which a human being can make some approach to knowing the whole of a subject is by hearing what can be said about it by persons of every variety of opinion and studying all modes in which it can be looked at by every character of mind. No wise man ever acquired his wisdom in any mode but this."*
>
> John Stuart Mill

In our media-intensive culture it is not difficult to find differing opinions. Thousands of newspapers and magazines and dozens of radio and television talk shows resound with differing points of view. The difficulty lies in deciding which opinion to agree with and which "experts" seem the most credible. The more inundated we become with differing opinions and claims, the more essential it is to hone critical reading and thinking skills to evaluate these ideas. Opposing Viewpoints books address this problem directly by presenting stimulating debates that can be used to enhance and teach these skills. The varied opinions contained in each book examine many different aspects of a single issue. While examining these conveniently edited opposing views, readers can develop critical thinking skills such as the ability to compare and contrast authors' credibility, facts, argumentation styles, use of persuasive techniques, and other stylistic tools. In short, the Opposing Viewpoints Series is an ideal way to attain the higher-level thinking and reading skills so essential in a culture of diverse and contradictory opinions.

In addition to providing a tool for critical thinking, Opposing Viewpoints books challenge readers to question their own strongly held opinions and assumptions. Most people form their opinions on the basis of upbringing, peer pressure, and personal, cultural, or professional bias. By reading carefully balanced opposing views, readers must directly confront new ideas as well as the opinions of those with whom they disagree. This is not to argue simplistically that everyone who reads opposing views will—or should—change his or her opinion. Instead, the series enhances readers' understanding of their own views by encouraging confrontation with opposing ideas. Careful examination of others' views can lead to the readers' understanding of the logical inconsistencies in their own opinions, perspective on why they hold an opinion, and the consideration of the possibility that their opinion requires further evaluation.

Evaluating Other Opinions

To ensure that this type of examination occurs, Opposing Viewpoints books present all types of opinions. Prominent spokespeople on different sides of each issue as well as well-known professionals from many disciplines challenge the reader. An additional goal of the series is to provide a forum for other, less known, or even unpopular viewpoints. The opinion of an ordinary person who has had to make the decision to cut off life support from a terminally ill relative, for example, may be just as valuable and provide just as much insight as a medical ethicist's professional opinion. The editors have two additional purposes in including these less known views. One, the editors encourage readers to respect others' opinions—even when not enhanced by professional credibility. It is only by reading or listening to and objectively evaluating others' ideas that one can determine whether they are worthy of consideration. Two, the inclusion of such viewpoints encourages the important critical thinking skill of objectively evaluating an author's credentials and bias. This evaluation will illuminate an author's reasons for taking a particular stance on an issue and will aid in readers' evaluation of the author's ideas.

It is our hope that these books will give readers a deeper understanding of the issues debated and an appreciation of the complexity of even seemingly simple issues when good and honest people disagree. This awareness is particularly important in a democratic society such as ours in which people enter into public debate to determine the common good. Those with whom one disagrees should not be regarded as enemies but rather as people whose views deserve careful examination and may shed light on one's own.

Thomas Jefferson once said that "difference of opinion leads to inquiry, and inquiry to truth." Jefferson, a broadly educated man, argued that "if a nation expects to be ignorant and free . . . it expects what never was and never will be." As individuals and as a nation, it is imperative that we consider the opinions of others and examine them with skill and discernment. The Opposing Viewpoints series is intended to help readers achieve this goal.

David L. Bender and Bruno Leone,
Founders

Introduction

> *"No woman can call herself free who does not own and control her body. No woman can call herself free until she can choose consciously whether she will or will not be a mother."*
>
> —*Margaret Sanger,*
> *"The Right to One's Body," 1920*

Throughout history, men and women have utilized a wide range of methods to gain some control over reproduction. Some of these birth control methods were primitive and ineffective; others were based on folklore and false notions. Some were dangerous and put the lives of young women in danger. Some taken from herbs and plants were surprisingly efficacious. The evolution of birth control throughout the centuries is a testament to the important role it has played in human life and the universal desire of women to control their own bodies. Exploring the history of this evolution inspires an appreciation for the highly advanced, safe, and regulated methods men and women have at their disposal today.

In ancient cultures, many of the popular birth control methods were harmful and could result in permanent physical damage and even death. Centuries ago, for example, Chinese women drank lead and mercury as birth control, often resulting in death. Ancient Greek women ate pennyroyal leaves, which could be toxic, to avoid pregnancy. One safe plant used for birth control was silphium, which was found only in Libya. It proved to be so effective that it was overharvested and became extinct by the fourth century. In ancient Egypt, women used cotton tampons soaked in the fermented juice of acacia plants. Women in tropical climates, particularly Sri Lanka and some parts of India, eat a papaya a day as a contraceptive. In

1993 researchers discovered that an enzyme in the fruit interacts with the hormone progesterone, successfully preventing pregnancy.

Some methods that women used were based on magic or superstition, like the medieval practice of walking three times around the spot where a pregnant wolf had urinated. Another popular form of birth control in the Middle Ages was creating an amulet out of a hare's anus or a black cat's desiccated liver to wear around a woman's neck. In the Stone Ages, people thought that the spirits of babies lived in certain fruits, so eating those fruits would cause a woman to get pregnant. Years ago in New Brunswick, Canada, women drank a potion made of dried beaver testicle brewed in alcohol as a contraceptive.

Although people in past eras lacked the scientific knowledge that we have today, some cultures, such as Native American and African societies, did have a working understanding of the rhythms of a woman's body—especially the right times to abstain from sexual activity. Women came to understand early on that abstinence, especially at certain times of the month, was an effective form of birth control. Today, abstinence is taught and encouraged in many cultures, particularly for young, unmarried women.

Other methods we use today can be traced back to earlier cultures. For example, withdrawal has been a consistently popular form of birth control. There is even an example of withdrawal in the Bible in the story of Onan. Although ancient peoples did not know what sperm was, many cultures understood the connection between ejaculation and pregnancy. Many women also realized that breastfeeding was an effective method of birth control, because menstruation and ovulation are postponed while a woman is breastfeeding a child.

The condom is another birth control method that has been used for centuries, although men used it primarily to protect themselves from venereal disease. A three-thousand-year-old illustration of a man using a condom was found in Egypt. In France, researchers found a cave painting of a man wearing a condom during sex that is thought to be twelve to fifteen thousand years old. Archeologists have discovered condoms made of animal guts in the foundations of Dudley Castle in England. Experts speculate the condoms date back to 1640 and were used by soldiers fighting in the English Civil War. For years, condoms were made from a variety of materials, including linen, lamb intestines, and animal bladders. In the fifteenth century, Dutch traders sold condoms made of leather. By the eighteenth century, condoms were widely accessible and emerging as one of the most popular forms of birth control in the world. In 1855 the first rubber condom was manufactured. Latex condoms were first produced in 1920.

The great strides made in the birth control movement in the twentieth century can be attributed to one woman: Margaret Sanger. Widely regarded as the founder of the modern birth control movement, Sanger was an American reformer and educator who championed research of new birth control methods and the accessibility of birth control to women of all socioeconomic levels and races. Sanger's work was rooted in her own childhood, when she watched her mother get pregnant eighteen times in twenty-two years and die at the age of forty-five. Sanger believed that it was essential for women to have more control over family planning decisions and their own bodies. In 1916 she opened the first birth control clinic in the United States. Her arrest and prosecution for distributing contraceptives led to a court decision that allowed doctors to prescribe contraception to their patients. In 1921 she founded the American Birth Control League, which later became the Planned Parenthood Federation of America. In the early 1950s, she was instrumental in finding the resources to develop the oral contraceptive for women, also known as the birth control pill. Sanger found two doctors, John Rock and Gregory Pincus, who developed a birth control pill utilizing synthetic progesterone. The US Food and Drug Administration (FDA) approved the drug in 1957—but only for severe menstrual disorders, not for contraceptive reasons. It wasn't until 1960 that the FDA approved it for contraceptive use.

Within a few years of its arrival on the market, millions of American women were using the birth control pill. Other methods of contraception are also popular. First developed in Europe in the mid-nineteenth century, diaphragms are still widely used. During the twentieth century, the contraceptive sponge, the female condom, and the intrauterine device (IUD) hit the market. Today, new technologies are in the works, including a male birth control pill. With the constant advancement of scientific and medical knowledge, birth control technology will continue to move forward and provide safe, easy, and effective options for both women and men.

The authors of the viewpoints presented in *Opposing Viewpoints: Birth Control* explore the impact that birth control has on society in the following chapters: How Has Birth Control Affected Society?, What Impact Does the Birth Control Pill Have on Society?, How Should Access to Birth Control Be Managed?, and What Is the Best Approach to Birth Control and Sex Education for Teens? The information in this volume examines the moral, environmental, and societal implications of birth control and the ways government and society should control access to birth control for adults and teenagers.

OPPOSING
VIEWPOINTS®
SERIES

CHAPTER 1

How Has Birth Control Affected Society?

Chapter Preface

Emergency oral contraception is a safe way to prevent unplanned pregnancies after unprotected sexual intercourse. Better known as the morning-after pill, it has been an extremely popular option for women in parts of the world in which it is available. Depending on the type of morning-after pill, it can be taken hours or even days after intercourse and prevents pregnancy from occurring. According to Planned Parenthood, "All brands of the morning-after pill work by keeping a woman's ovaries from releasing eggs—ovulation. Pregnancy cannot happen if there is no egg to join with sperm. The hormone in the morning-after pill also prevents pregnancy by thickening a woman's cervical mucus. The mucus blocks sperm and keeps it from joining with an egg. The morning-after pill can also thin the lining of the uterus. In theory, this could prevent pregnancy by keeping a fertilized egg from attaching to the uterus."

The history of emergency contraception can be traced back to the 1920s, when researchers proved that the hormone known as estrogen prevented pregnancy in mammals. Veterinarians were the first to apply this research by giving horses and dogs doses of estrogen after they had mated with inappropriate partners. In the 1940s, there were reports that gynecologists were giving it to their patients after unplanned sex, but the first documented cases of using emergency contraception on humans weren't until the 1960s. The first known case was a doctor in the Netherlands who provided a dose of estrogen to prevent pregnancy in a thirteen-year-old girl who had been raped.

In 1966 a synthetic form of estrogen was developed by Dr. John McLean Morris. Eight years later, a Canadian doctor, A. Albert Yuzpe, formulated a method of emergency contraception that combined synthetic estrogen and progestin hormones. Called the Yuzpe regimen, it became the dominant method of emergency contraception during the 1980s. A woman on the Yuzpe regimen would start taking two doses of hormones, twelve hours apart, as soon as she could after having unprotected intercourse.

By the late 1990s, many countries were looking to transition to progestin-only emergency contraception instead of estrogen-progestin combinations. On July 28, 1999, the US Food and Drug Administration (FDA) approved Plan B, a progestin-only oral contraceptive for emergency use. Plan B quickly became a dominant brand in the US market.

Reproductive health advocates began to push for faster access to emergency contraception like Plan B. In many cases, women had to wait to see their doctors to get a prescription for Plan B—and with emergency contraception, the less time it takes to start the regimen, the more effective it will be. On August 24, 2006, the FDA gave its approval for women eighteen or older to have over-the-counter access to Plan B from pharmacies staffed by licensed pharmacists. This meant that adult women could buy it without a doctor's prescription, allowing them to start emergency contraception faster. Young women under the age of eighteen would still require a doctor's prescription.

Yet there was a renewed push to make Plan B more accessible. On March 23, 2009, a US judge ordered the FDA to allow seventeen-year-old girls to purchase Plan B without a doctor's prescription. The FDA complied. The change enraged conservative groups, who argued that seventeen-year-olds were too young to be using emergency contraception without consulting a doctor.

On August 16, 2010, the FDA announced its approval of ella as an emergency contraception in the United States. Birth control advocates hailed the arrival of ella because it successfully reduces the chance of pregnancy up to five days after unprotected sex. In contrast, Plan B has to be taken within three days after unprotected sex for it to be effective.

Antiabortion activists criticized the availability of ella, contending that because it can eliminate an embryo that has been implanted in a woman's uterus, it eliminates what could be a viable pregnancy. These activists argue that ella is more like mifepristone, or RU-486, known as the abortion pill, than Plan B.

The controversy over emergency contraception is one of the subjects covered in the following chapter, which examines the impact that birth control has had on society. Other viewpoints explore the question of how birth control has affected the number of abortions in the country, whether birth control has been beneficial to women and society, and the moral implications of taking Plan B or ella.

*"While feminist theory can be separated
into various strands . . . and various
waves . . . virtually all feminists would
place women's ability to control our
own bodies as a central tenet."*

Birth Control Asserts Feminist Values and Is Socially Beneficial

Naomi Cahn and June Carbone

*Naomi Cahn is a professor at the George Washington University
Law School. June Carbone is a law professor at the University of
Missouri-Kansas City School of Law. In the following viewpoint,
the authors maintain that access to contraception has enhanced
women's lives by providing autonomy and control over their reproductive choices. This, in turn, has helped increasing numbers
of teens and young women move into the middle class and
greater economic security. Nevertheless, Cahn and Carbone note,
access to contraception is perceived as a threat by social conservatives who are constantly trying to limit women's access to con-*

Naomi Cahn and June Carbone, "Contraception: Securing Feminism's Promise," *The
George Washington University Law School Public Law and Legal Theory Working Paper*,
July 2009, vol. 476, pp. 1–3, 9–13. Copyright © 2009 by Naomi Cahn and June Carbone.

traception. To protect all women's access to contraception, Cahn and Carbone maintain, the law has and will continue to play a key role.

As you read, consider the following questions:

1. According to Cahn and Carbone, what percentage of sexually active Americans will use contraception at some point in their lives?

2. What percentage of Americans do the authors say will have had sex outside of marriage by the age of forty-four?

3. In what year did Congress amend Title X to ensure that adolescents had access to family planning services?

For many young women, the first trip to Planned Parenthood, a Title X clinic, or a gynecologist is an important rite of passage. Some go with a parent. Some go because they think they *might* have sex. Many go for the first time because they think they are already pregnant. Others go because they are married and not ready for children—or for more than [they] already have.

Contraception is an issue where the law can matter. Feminist advocacy for reproductive rights nicely shows, in the words of the conference, how feminist legal theory is changing, and has changed, the law. Yet, we're not done: Women's reproductive rights remain under attack. We want to use this to explore one complex aspect of feminist legal theory: One core strength of much of feminist legal theory is an emphasis on contextual legal reasoning and attention to relationships, while another strength is the feminist challenge to rethink existing frameworks. The two may collide when feminists engage with contraceptive opponents, who seek to define the debate. The answer here is not compromise, but reframing, potentially at the expense of engagement. For example, several years ago, NARAL Pro-Choice America placed an ad in the *Weekly Stan-*

dard, a conservative magazine, asking antichoice activists to join with it in programs to decrease the need for abortions. A noble effort to form a coalition? A waste of money? "[T]actical skepticism [that] can leave people blind to real danger"?

The Politics of Feminist Discourse

Feminists are often good at coloring within the lines. We build alliances, we work within existing frameworks, we are sensitive to nuance, we want things that seem reasonable and commonsensical—at least once the world acknowledges women's perspectives. Are we out of place in a polarized political universe? That is, in an era where one side seizes on the very words "family planning" as a situs [position] of political controversy and the other side caves without protest, have our tactics been proven bankrupt? Or is the failure simply a return to the norm; a norm in which women's interests are marginalized and invisible? In this [viewpoint], we will return to an issue associated with the modern women's movement: contraception. We will argue that this issue combines the two halves of feminist strategy. To prevail requires a reframing of the existing political discourse and the reframing turns on once again making women's issues, variety, and needs visible in the political arena.

The Law and Access to Contraception

Access to contraception is an arena in which law plays an important role. Legal changes secured the initial access to the pill, whose distribution was initially illegal throughout most of the United States. It won the extension of the right to contraception to the unmarried, a right that would have had difficulty passing muster in state legislatures. Constitutional rulings further secured access for minors, keeping pathways to middle-class status open for increasing numbers of teens. Yet, these victories, which have enhanced women's autonomy and material well-being, have also been deeply threatening to traditional ideologies, both ideologies about family and about the control of sexuality. The alliance of conservative family values with conservative business interests has in turn created a political climate that threatens to once again marginalize women's interests.

The legal fights over what forms of contraception are permissible, who has access and under what circumstances, are fundamentally about control of the socialization of the next generation. The much more divisive (and seemingly principled) issue of abortion receives the lion's share of publicity and anger, but contraception has been, and remains, a hidden casualty of the conflict. It is also an issue ripe for reframing—and for making the subterranean assaults on women's interests visible. While feminist theory can be separated into various strands—liberal, radical, dominance, reconstructive—and various waves—first, second, and third—virtually all feminists would place women's ability to control our own bodies as a central tenet. Moreover, if there is any issue that should be able to rally consensus support with the general public, it should be the principle of reducing unwanted pregnancies. We believe that both abstinence and abortion are distracters in this effort; the critical issue is the availability and affordability of birth control. Over 95% of sexually active Americans will use contraception at some point in their lives, over 90% of Americans will engage in nonmarital sexuality, and over 60% agree that sexuality outside of marriage is permissible. Moreover, unlike abortion, there is little objection to contraception per se, with even 75% of Catholics agreeing that the Church's position on birth control should be changed.

Protecting the Vulnerable

Yet, amidst controversies over abstinence education in public schools and the continuing abortion wars, the class-based nature of contraceptive access has become invisible. We explore the hypocrisy of a system that, whatever its values, makes reproductive autonomy readily available for the affluent and the sophisticated and increasingly beyond the reach of the most vulnerable. We also consider the potential of contraception as a reframing device, capable of exposing the hypocrisy of family-values advocates whose policies disproportionately hurt the most vulnerable. This [viewpoint] traces the history of attempts to restrict contraception, the legal events securing widespread access to contraception and their importance to a generation of college-aged women, the short-lived nature of the consensus that produced them, and the potential of the issue to serve as a rallying point for a revitalized feminism. . . .

Contraception for the Masses

The advent of birth control did more, of course, than simply enhance the careers and marriage prospects of college educated women. It changed the norms and attitudes of society as a whole toward sexual activity—and toward women's autonomy. The figures we cited earlier that indicate that the percent of the population having sex by the age of 21 rose from 40% to 70% were for the entire population. Today, 77% of men and women will have had sex, including 75% who will have had premarital sex, by the age of 20. By the age of 44, 95% of the entire population will have had sex outside of marriage, and they will overwhelmingly have done so with someone other than a person they will eventually marry. Public attitudes toward nonmarital sexuality have shifted with the change in practices; 61% of adults aged 18 to 29 approve of premarital sex today compared with 21% of the same group in a Gallup poll in 1969.

Acceptance of nonmarital sexuality also meant, at least for a brief period, a willingness to consider its consequences. Political proposals for greater family planning assistance date back decades. In the fifties, however, President [Dwight D.] Eisenhower dismissed them, observing that he could not "imagine anything more emphatically a subject that is not a proper political or governmental activity or function or responsibility.... This government will not, as long as I am here, have a positive political doctrine in its program that has to do with this problem of birth control. That is not our business." By the mid-sixties, however, the discourse on contraception more generally came together with greater concern about poverty, and a racialized discourse about fertility.

Perhaps the most influential study of fertility in the sixties indicated that while poor women had dramatically higher fertility rates than the affluent (one report compared the birth rates of the Chicago urban poor to those in India), poor women and minority women actually wanted fewer children than the affluent, and twice as many of the children born to the poor were unwanted in comparison with the children born to better-off mothers. The study found, for example, that 17% of whites and 31% of blacks had not wanted the last child born to them. For those women who had not completed high school, the figures were even higher, with 31% of whites and 43% of blacks stating that their last child had not been wanted. The two-tiered system produced by the Comstock laws, in which the sophisticated secured effective birth control, where the less advantaged did not, had a palpable effect on fertility rates.

The War on Poverty

The discussion of fertility came as President [Lyndon B.] Johnson was launching a war on poverty, and as the Supreme Court was eliminating the last vestiges of the moral regulations that excluded poor women from welfare eligibility. When Congress authorized the aid to dependent children program in the thirties, it designed the program primarily for widows and allowed the states to bar nonmarital children from benefits. By the sixties, the federal agency charged with oversight of the program had eliminated most of the formal prohibitions, but it continued to deem the income of males present

History of the Birth Control Pill

In 1948, Planned Parenthood had awarded a small grant to Gregory Pincus, a research biologist who undertook a series of tests leading to the development of the birth control pill. On May 9, 1960, the U.S. Food and Drug Administration (FDA) [approved] the sale of oral pills for contraception. The pill [was] an instant hit and has [had] enormous consequences in freeing women to control their lives. Finally women [had] an easy and reliable means to prevent unwanted pregnancies and plan their families.

Within five years, one out of every four married women in America under the age of 45 [had] used the pill.

"History & Successes,"
Planned Parenthood, 2011.
www.plannedparenthood.org.

in the home available to the family. To check up on the presence of such unreported cohabitants, welfare authorities conducted midnight visits, dubbed "Operation Bedcheck," to determine continued eligibility. In 1968, the Supreme Court ruled that such practices were inconsistent with the statutory scheme. It explained that "Congress has determined that immorality and illegitimacy should be dealt with through rehabilitative measures rather than measures that punish dependent children." The Court found it "simply inconceivable" that any state would be free "to discourage immorality and illegitimacy by the device of absolute disqualification of needy children."

As a result of active outreach as part of the war on poverty and the relaxation of the restrictions, welfare ranks swelled. In the early to mid-sixties, only half of those who were eligible received welfare benefits. By 1976, however, the number of families participating in the welfare program increased from less than a million in 1964 to 3.5 million, more than tripling the size of the program. Moreover, while the majority of welfare recipients have always been white, African Americans are dramatically more likely than whites to be poor. The percentage of African American beneficiaries increased steadily through the sixties and early seventies, peaking in 1976, with blacks at 46% of the caseload, even though they constituted only 11% of the population. During the same period, concern grew about the changing composition of the African American family, with nonmarital births growing from 25% of the total in 1965 (the time of the Moynihan report, which touched off a political firestorm by calling attention to the high numbers) to 60% by 1975.

The Importance of Family Planning

In this context, calls for increased access to family planning services won bipartisan support. Kristin Luker reports that: "When poor women were having unwanted, out-of-wedlock births in such large numbers (out-of-wedlock births were assumed to be unwanted births), and when unwanted babies seemed to [be] swelling the AFDC [Aid to Families with Dependent Children] rolls, an archaic birth control policy that kept contraceptives out of the hands of the poor seemed ludicrous, if not tragic." It probably did not hurt politically that the Supreme Court's birth control decision in *Griswold [v. Connecticut]* had drawn little protest, and that the major skeptics of the new proposals were black nationalists who saw the emphasis on birth control for poor black women as a form of genocide.

In 1966—6 years before the Supreme Court's decision in *Eisenstadt [v. Baird]* extending the right to contraception to single women and years before the Court's decision providing access to adolescents—a bipartisan congressional committee recommended that publicly funded birth control be made available to any AFDC recipient over the age of 15, regardless of whether she was married. Congress also made contraception a special emphasis of the war on poverty, appropriating specific funds for family planning efforts. In 1970, Congress passed and President Richard Nixon signed Title X of the Public Health Service Act, which created "a comprehensive federal program devoted entirely to the provision of family planning services on a national basis." The vote was unanimous in the Senate and overwhelming in the House (298–32). Two years later, at the insistence of the Nixon administration, Congress amended the Medicaid statute to add family planning to the list of "mandated services" that health care providers must provide in order to remain eligible for federal Medicaid funds. Even more remarkably, by the late seventies, Congress agreed that adolescent sexuality was an important concern and, in 1978, in the year following the Supreme Court's insistence that teen access to contraception could not be conditioned on parental consent, Congress amended Title X to make it clear that recipients of Title X family planning funds were *required* to provide services to adolescents. Family planning had become central to Democratic *and* Republican antipoverty efforts, and been transformed in the words of one historian from "private vice to public virtue."

Gender Equality Is Temporarily Triumphant

The emergence of what we are today calling the blue family paradigm was neither partisan nor ideological, though parts of it were certainly controversial. It reflected the convergence of the interests of a favored group—middle-class college students—with concerns about the "excess fertility" of a disfavored group—the urban poor. Moreover, the most practical assertion of the new paradigm—support for contraception—

was intensely pragmatic. Middle-class women, whether married or single, had embraced the pill in overwhelming numbers, and opposition was politically perilous. At the same time, making the same means available for poorer women simply made sense, whether the support was motivated by concern for reproductive autonomy or for reducing the numbers of a group viewed as a drain on societal resources.

At the center of these developments, however, were important principles that allowed a reformulation of family practices. Critical among them was the idea that childbirth should be chosen, rather than an inevitable or punitive consequence of sexual activity. This idea commanded overwhelming support both in the congressional votes for family planning, and in the Supreme Court cases that extended the right to privacy to single individuals and teens. The idea was both substantive (at its core is a commitment to reproductive autonomy), and pragmatic (the alternatives were proven failures as the numbers of unwanted pregnancies attested). It was also an essential component in women's greater autonomy.

The Court in both *Eisenstadt* and *Carey v. Population Services [International]*, the case that invalidated the New York law restricting distribution of contraceptives to minors, further rejected the asserted state interest in pregnancy as a deterrent to sexual activity as a legitimate basis of state regulation. In *Carey*, the state had argued that the availability of birth control would "lead to increased sexual activity among the young." Yet, the Court dismissed the suggestion that it is appropriate to deter sexual activity by "increasing the hazards attendant on it," observing that "no court or commentator has taken the argument seriously." The reason, which the *Eisenstadt* court had also recognized, was that: "It would be plainly unreasonable to assume that the [State] has prescribed pregnancy and the birth of an unwanted child as punishment for fornication. We remain reluctant to attribute any such 'scheme of values' to the State." With that declaration, the shotgun marriage as official state policy was at an end—at least until the next decade brought it back.

> *"The contraceptive revolution has re-sulted in a massive redistribution of wealth and power from women and children to men."*

Birth Control Is a Sexist Practice and Damaging to Society

Timothy Reichert

Timothy Reichert is an economist and a writer. In the following viewpoint, he argues that the widespread popularity of birth control has caused men to become more powerful and wealthy and women and children to lose social influence and economic security. This shift has been profoundly detrimental to the social and economic standing of women, Reichert contends. The author maintains that contraception has divided women and men into sex and marriage markets, with men holding most of the power in the marriage market. This forces women to settle for less power and financial security in marriage and has led to more divorce, infidelity, and marital dissatisfaction.

As you read, consider the following questions:

1. According to Betsey Stevenson and Justin Wolfers, how far did the percentage of Americans married at age thirty fall from 1960 to 2000?

2. In which mating market—sex or marriage—does the author say that women have more power?

3. What does the author say has been the ultimate result of women moving into the labor market?

Economists and other social scientists have written extensively about the impact that contraception has had on modern sexual relationships. Almost without exception, the academic establishment makes the claim that contraceptive technology is a social good. By contrast, the Catholic Church (and until recent decades the Christian establishment generally) asserts that the practice of contraception is, in fact, directly contrary to the health of individual families and to society as a whole.

The difference between these two perspectives on an issue that is central to human sexuality—and therefore human existence—is striking. But meaningful debate between the two camps has been almost nonexistent. Certainly, part of the reason for this has been an unwillingness on the part of secular social scientists to engage in honest dialogue. But an equally large part of the blame for the nonengagement should be laid at the feet of Catholics. With a few notable exceptions, the Catholic perspective has not been taken seriously by Catholics themselves. Nor, in the cases when it has, has it been articulated using the language of social science, which is the language of the mainstream. As a result, the difference in viewpoint on an issue that is central to the human person is treated by our culture as a case of faith and reason talking past each other.

With this [viewpoint], using the language and tools of modern social science, I will articulate the position that contraception is socially damaging. I will also demonstrate that contraception is in fact a sexist practice. Using straightforward microeconomic reasoning, I will unpack the behaviors engendered by artificial contraception. I will show that the contraceptive revolution has resulted in a massive redistribution of wealth and power from women and children to men.

In doing so, I will reveal that despite the ethical inferiority of artificial contraception, the practice of contraception will, unfortunately, predominate as the social "equilibrium" unless legal restrictions or social mores "tax" men and "subsidize" women and children. More technically, artificial contraception sets up what economists call a "prisoner's dilemma" game, in which each woman is induced to make decisions rationally that ultimately make her, and all women, worse off. This result is particularly striking and has broad implications for how we think about the sexual revolution and its aftermath.

The Basic Economics of Contraception

Economists view social phenomena through the lens of markets. This does not mean that economists believe that all social interaction is, in fact, coordinated through explicit cash pricing. Rather, it means that economists recognize that relative scarcity or abundance affects behavior in important ways.

Economists are trained to use a set of reasoning tools to identify and explain the sometimes subtle ways in which, for example, new technologies (such as chemical contraception) or other fundamental changes unfold themselves into much broader social dynamics.

What are the social processes that should be logically included under the rubric of contraception? First and foremost, contraception divides what was once a single mating "market," wherein men and women paired in marriage, into two separate markets—a market for sexual relationships that most people now frequent during the early phase of their adult life-times (I will refer to this as the "sex market"), and a market for marital relationships that is inhabited during the later phases (I will refer to this as the "marriage market").

Obviously, contraceptive technology provides the assurance that participation in the sex market will not result in pregnancy. It therefore lowers the costs of premarital and extramarital sexual activity below the level necessary for a separate sex market to form.

Participation in the Marriage Market

Data compiled by Betsey Stevenson and Justin Wolfers of the Wharton School at the University of Pennsylvania show a marked decrease in participation in the marriage market, at ages 15 to 60, over the forty-year period from 1960 to 2000. Their graph . . . shows that, for example, the percentage of Americans married at age 30 fell from roughly 85 percent in 1960 to roughly 60 percent in 2000. Assuming that sexual activity has not decreased over the same period (clearly a safe assumption), this implies increased participation in the sex market over the same period.

Work by Harvard economists Claudia Goldin and Lawrence Katz bears this out. Their graphs show a marked decrease over time in women's participation in the marriage market at ages 20 through 30, and a corresponding increase in their participation in the sex market.

This separation of a single mating market into two separate markets—the sex market and the marriage market—is not necessarily adverse to either women or men. It is only when imbalances exist in these markets that the "price" of either marriage or sex tilts in favor of one or the other gender. In other words, whereas the marriage market was, by definition, populated by roughly the same number of men as women, there is no guarantee that once it has been separated into two markets, men and women will sort themselves into the sex and marriage markets in such a way that roughly equal numbers of each gender will inhabit each market.

It may be biologically inevitable that relatively more men will populate the sex market and relatively more women will populate the marriage market. The reason for this is simple. The vast majority of women want to have children sometime during their lives. This can happen only before menopause, and if women want to ensure higher levels of fitness for their children, it should happen well before that. Further, prospective mothers recognize that stable marriage is far more preferable for the well-being of their children than is cohabitation or single parenting. This means that before a certain age— usually sometime in their early thirties at the latest—most women will inhabit the marriage market rather than the sex market.

By contrast, men face no such constraints. Men can reproduce at very late stages in their life cycle. This means that men do not face the same time pressure that women do to move out of the sex market and into the marriage market.

Men vs. Women

The notion that more men than women will populate the sex market is also supported by evolutionary biology—a field closely related to microeconomics. Men and women have different approaches to sex and marriage. Women take nine months to make a baby, while it takes a man about ten minutes. As the evolutionary biologist Robert Trivers has pointed out, this simple biological fact, in conjunction with the force of natural selection, lies behind the commonsense notion that males are always available for sex. Men invest very little to spread their genes. For females, by contrast, sex leads to pregnancy, which leads to a lifelong commitment of time and resources.

The implications are straightforward. The average age at which men exit the sex market and enter the marriage market is higher than the average age at which women make the same decision. This, in turn, means that at each point in time, more men will inhabit the sex market than women. Correspondingly, more women will inhabit the marriage market than men.

A Changing Picture for Women

The result is easy to see. From the perspective of women, the sex market is one in which they have more bargaining power than men. They are the scarce commodity in this market and can command higher "prices" than men while inhabiting it.

But the picture is very different once these same women make the switch to the marriage market. The relative scarcity of marriageable men means that the competition among women for marriageable men is far fiercer than that faced by prior generations of women. Over time, this means that the "deals they cut" become worse for them and better for men.

The institution of marriage shifts from an institution that was motivated (at least in part) by the need to protect and foster women and the children they bear, to an institution that is motivated more by what Stevenson and Wolfers call "joint consumption." In practice, this means that marriage moves from something resembling a contractual arrangement to something that is, instead, more frail and resembles a spot market exchange. The day-to-day aspects of marriage shift relatively toward the welfare of men, and relatively away from the welfare of women and their children. In short, men take more and more of the "gains from trade" that marriage creates, and women take fewer and fewer.

The Implications of Scarcity

The immediate implication of the separation of the mating market into sex and marriage markets is that women generally will have a strong bargaining position relative to men when coupling in the sex market, because of their relative scarcity, but later will have a weak relative bargaining position in the marriage market, because of the relative scarcity of men in this market.

This produces a redistribution of bargaining power and, ultimately, of welfare from the later child-rearing phases of a woman's lifetime toward the earlier, and in my view less important, phases. This redistribution has some very concrete, very undesirable consequences for women—and for the children that they bear.

Specifically, from the bifurcation of the mating market into separate sex and marriage markets come several self-reinforcing processes. Foremost among these is that contraception inevitably leads to more divorce.

Contraception and Divorce

There are two reasons for this. First, because of the lower relative bargaining power that women wield relative to men in the marriage market, at the margin more women will simply strike "bad deals" and will want a way out of the marital covenant *ex post* [based on prior experience]. In the era before contraception, roughly equal numbers of women and men in the marriage market meant that men and women roughly split the gains from trade that stem from marriage. By contrast, in the post-contraceptive era women give away many, indeed most, of these gains to men. This lower level of "surplus," or marital benefit, for women means that there is precious little room in the course of their marriages for downside. In other words, when things go wrong relative to what was expected, women who expected to be somewhat better off because of the gains from marriage now find themselves in a position of being *worse off* within marriage than they would have been as single persons. This, in turn, leads quite naturally to an increase in the demand for divorce *ex post*.

Second, there is a closely related "demand for divorce" *before* marriage even occurs. That is, there is now an *ex ante* [based on predicted future events] demand for divorce in the form of a premarriage exit option. In other words, women now demand, before marriage, an exit option just in case things turn out badly.

Divorce and the Social Stigma

At the level of culture, women demand this option by allowing the strictures and social mores surrounding divorce to erode. Divorce no longer carries with it any kind of stigma because the women among us who formerly would have created this stigma recognize that having the option is now in their interest, too.

At the level of politics women do the same by allowing, and sometimes organizing on behalf of, laws such as no-fault divorce laws. Rationally, instead of "burning their bridges" by irrevocably committing themselves, women today walk into the marriage covenant fundamentally less committed than women fifty years ago. And men have responded rationally by doing the same.

A Poor Trade-off

One important strategy that allows women both to create a safer exit for themselves and to increase their bargaining power going into a marriage is to develop relatively more market earning power—more market-rewarded human capital—than they would have in past decades. Thus, women have substituted labor market–rewarded human capital for human capital that earned its return in nonmonetary ways such as deeper and stronger familial relationships, mother-child relationships that result in better day-to-day moral formation of children, and community activism. . . .

The strategy is, in essence, to become more like men. Women today rarely specialize in the home, or in the family, but, rather, in marketable labor. By specializing in exactly the same thing, both men and women have eroded the gains from trade that potentially exist in marriage. That is, the principle of comparative advantage no longer applies, or at least does not apply with the same force as in the past. This, in turn, means that men and women become, quite simply, less interesting to one another. Sameness begets ennui, which begets divorce. Indeed, sexless ennui is cited as an important part of the reasoning that Sandra Tsing Loh gives for divorcing her husband in a heavily discussed 2009 article in the *Atlantic*.

Contraception and Investments

A second socioeconomic phenomenon that results from contraception involves the market for important household investments such as real estate. Real estate is a commodity that is naturally limited in supply. It therefore increases rapidly in price as wealthier two-earner households bid up the price of homes. At the margin, this forces yet more women into the labor market and reinforces the erosion of specialization in the home. In other words, the more couples that send the wife into the labor market, the more price pressure there is on other couples to do the same. A single-income family becomes less and less able to meet its basic needs as real estate and other supply-limited goods are increasingly priced at a two-income level.

This, too, represents a redistribution of welfare from younger to older generations, and from a family's younger, child-rearing years to its later, childless years. Buying land for $500,000 that otherwise would cost $300,000 means two things. First, a larger share of a young family's budget must go to mortgage-related interest payments instead of to education for the children—or, for that matter, to producing new children. This is the phenomenon of more expensive homes that house fewer people as the median family size falls. Second, families are, in essence, shifting wealth from their earlier years

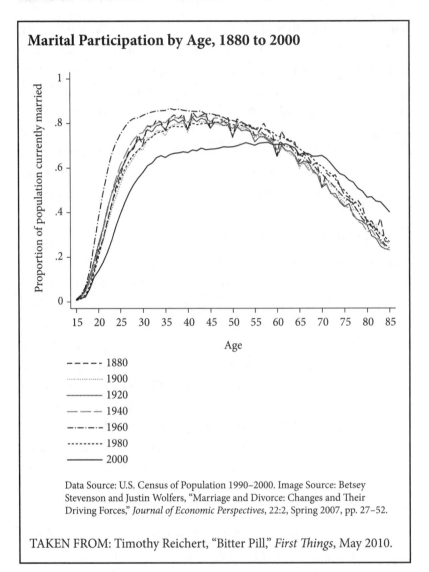

Marital Participation by Age, 1880 to 2000

Proportion of population currently married

- – – – – 1880
- ·············· 1900
- ▬▬▬▬ 1920
- – – – 1940
- –·–·–·– 1960
- ·········· 1980
- ▬▬▬▬ 2000

Data Source: U.S. Census of Population 1990–2000. Image Source: Betsey Stevenson and Justin Wolfers, "Marriage and Divorce: Changes and Their Driving Forces," *Journal of Economic Perspectives*, 22:2, Spring 2007, pp. 27–52.

TAKEN FROM: Timothy Reichert, "Bitter Pill," *First Things*, May 2010.

to their later years, when, they hope, they can sell the $500,000 house. This inter-temporal [related to past, present, and future] redistribution from younger to older phases of the family's life cycle rests largely on the backs of the women in the labor force who support the higher housing cost and, ultimately, on the children who otherwise would have had the benefits of their mothers' time.

Contraception and Infidelity

Contraception also increases the incidence of infidelity. The mechanisms that cause this are relatively obvious but worth mentioning here. First, contraception nearly eliminates the risk of conceiving a child with someone other than one's spouse, thereby eliminating most of the detection risk for the unfaithful. Further, the fact that contraception cleaves the marriage market into separate markets for sex and marriage creates a ready market for married individuals to dip into should they desire a tryst. Before contraception, it was prostitution—a market much more limited in size—that offered the primary opportunities for infidelity.

Focus-group research on African American women by Cynthia Woodsong and Helen Koo supports this claim. They find that increased use of contraception among African American women and their partners increases mistrust between the partners due to higher risk of infidelity.

Here again, we see a redistribution of welfare away from married women. Contraception lowers the cost of detection for both men and women who wish to engage in infidelity. But it lowers the cost of infidelity for women by more than it lowers the cost for men. For women, detection due to an unwanted pregnancy is far more costly than detection is for men; therefore elimination of this risk results in a greater cost reduction for women than for men. In theory, this should increase the demand for infidelity by married women more than it increases the demand by married men. But contraception also increases the relative "benefit" of infidelity to men by more than it does for women. This occurs because younger women in the sex market are more attracted to successful older men than younger men in the sex market are attracted to older women. In other words, contraception opens up more opportunities for infidelity to married men than it does for married women. My contention is that, on the whole, contraception increases the demand for infidelity by married men more than it increases the demand by married women.

Contraception and Abortion

Finally, contraception creates a demand for abortion. The negative ramifications of childbearing on labor-market participation for women, coupled with the segmentation of one's sexual life span into two phases, means that women rationally plan their human capital investments around child rearing during the later phases of their lives. Further, the ability to control pregnancy means that women, in particular, can now make human-capital investments that allow for careers that were previously unavailable to them. When, however, things go awry and threaten their investments, they demand abortions. The cost today of an unwanted pregnancy is not a shotgun wedding. Rather, the cost is the loss of tremendous investments in human capital geared toward labor-market participation during the early phases of one's life. This increases the demand for abortions (which prevent the loss of that human capital).

Contraception and abortion are complementary forms of insurance that resemble primary insurance and reinsurance. If contraception fails, abortion is there as a fail-safe. This implies that we should see in the data a rise in both contraceptive use and the incidence of abortion until equilibrium levels of sexual activity are reached, after which abortion rates should remain relatively constant.

In fact, the data roughly bear this out. . . . The rise in abortion after legalization was strongly correlated with the rise in the use of contraceptive technology.

The Costs of Abortion

The decrease in the abortion rate after the early 1980s may be related to greater public awareness of the nature of the abortion procedure. It may also be related to advances in contraceptive technology that make contraception (primary insurance) cheaper relative to abortion (secondary insurance). And, once again, women bear the cost—both monetarily and emotionally. The data show that when an abortion occurs, the woman typically pays for the procedure. And it is the woman, not the man, who bears the emotional costs of postabortion guilt and trauma.

By now, it should be clear to the reader that, in my view, contraception is, contrary to the rhetoric of the sexual revolution, deeply sexist in nature. Contraception has resulted in an enormous redistribution of welfare from women to men, as well as an inter-temporal redistribution of welfare from a typical woman's later, child-rearing years to her earlier years.

Further, given that women's welfare largely determines the welfare of children, this redistribution has in part been "funded" by a loss of welfare from children. In other words, the worse off are women, the worse off are the children they support. On net, women and children are the big losers in the contraceptive society.

This thesis is consistent with the empirical evidence that exists relating to women's happiness. In a 2009 article, Stevenson and Wolfers show that over the past thirty-five years

> measures of subjective well-being indicate that women's happiness has declined both absolutely and relative to men. The paradox of women's declining relative well-being is found across various data sets, measures of subjective well-being, and is pervasive across demographic groups and industrialized countries. Relative declines in female happiness have eroded a gender gap in happiness in which women in the 1970s typically reported higher subjective well-being than did men. These declines have continued and a new gender gap is emerging—one with higher subjective well-being for men.

[Data] show just how sharp the decline in the relative happiness of women has been over the period of the sexual revolution. The bottom panel, in particular, uses an econometric technique to derive the trend in the relative happiness of women—a measure of the way in which men and women share the gains from trade of their unions.

Stevenson and Wolfers' interpretation of the data is striking.

> To compare this change with other well-known shifters of the happiness distribution, we can consider how large an increase in unemployment would be needed to generate a similar shift in subjective well-being. In a related context, Wolfers (2003) regressed individual happiness measures against a state's unemployment rate, controlling for state and year fixed effects, finding that a one percentage point rise in a state's unemployment rate leads to a decline in happiness of 0.015 points. The ratio between these two estimates suggests that the relative decline in the subjective well-being of U.S. women over the past thirty-five years is roughly comparable to the effects of an 8.5 percentage point rise in unemployment (that is, a rise from, say 4 percent unemployment to 12.5 percent). . . . Across a range of ordered probit regressions of happiness or life satisfaction on the log of GDP [gross domestic product] per capital, Wolfers (2006) finds coefficient estimates of around 0.2, suggesting that the relative decline in women's well-being over the past 35 years is equivalent to them having enjoyed *none* [emphasis added] of the accumulated gains due to economic growth.

The impact of this redistribution of welfare is profound—and alarming. Societies are structured around many objectives, but one of their chief reasons to be is the protection of the weak. This means the old, the young, and childbearing and child-rearing women. Contraception undermines this fundamental imperative, and, in so doing, undermines the legitimacy of the social contract. When the social fabric of a society is geared to move welfare from the weak to the strong, rather than the other way around, it cannot survive in the long run.

> *"Planned Parenthood has been distributing more and more contraception for 40+ years and yet continues to break new records in the number of abortions it performs each year."*

Birth Control Has Resulted in an Increase in Abortions

Thomas Peters

Thomas Peters is a writer for the American Papist *blog at CatholicVote.org. In the following viewpoint, he observes that the accepted Planned Parenthood assertion that more and better access to contraception leads to fewer abortions is wrong. In fact, Peters argues, despite increased funding and the distribution of more and more contraception to young women, the number of abortions that Planned Parenthood performs continues to increase. He contends that contraception does not bring down the abortion rate because it fails to prevent pregnancy on a consistent basis; it creates a culture of risky sex; and it is already widely accessible in American society.*

As you read, consider the following questions:

1. According to Peters, who was the liberal author who dared take on the proabortion orthodoxy?

2. How does contraception create an atmosphere of risky sex, according to the author?

3. According to Peters, what is Planned Parenthood's main mission?

Kirsten Powers did a brave thing.

Despite her liberal views, she dared to challenge the pro-abortion orthodoxy which holds that *even more contraception* is the answer (and in fact, the only answer) to the "high number of abortions" performed every year.

Last week [March 4, 2011] she wrote an article for the *Daily Beast* entitled "Busting the Birth-Control Myth" where she attempted to take on the Planned Parenthood orthodoxy.

The Predictable Counterattack

Their response was predictable: a swift and relentless counterattack. This is because the pro-aborts understand that "more contraception = less abortions" is the last argument they have to justify what they do.

Their argument goes like this: "So you don't like abortion? Fine, give us more money to give out more contraception . . . and then there will be less abortions." I've heard this canned line *ad nauseum* [continued to the point of nausea], whenever Planned Parenthood is asked to respond to the latest report on the growing number of abortions.

Luckily, the pro-aborts found a gap in Powers's argument: She got the year wrong on *one* of the studies she quoted. She was subsequently forced to write a retraction which concluded, "*I am deeply sorry for the error, which invalidates my piece.*"

Powers's Point Stands

One tiny problem ... her error does not invalidate her biggest point:

> To preserve its federal subsidy, Planned Parenthood continues to claim that without its contraception services the abortion rate will go up. This deception smacks of a fleecing of taxpayers in an effort to promote an ideological agenda, rather than a sincere effort to help women plan families.

In point of fact, Planned Parenthood's claims about contraception reducing the abortion rate *are* false, as Michael New argues [in the *National Review Online*, March 9, 2011] in depth:

> A look at the existing research on contraception use and abortion rates indicates that Powers's argument was stronger than she probably realizes.
>
> ... For many years, the mainstream media has subjected Planned Parenthood's claims about the benefits of federal contraception funding to precious little scrutiny. That is why it was so heartening to see someone not affiliated with the pro-life movement do some research and publicly document the shortcomings in Planned Parenthood's arguments. Even in light of the error, nearly all the research Powers presented was correct and damaging to Planned Parenthood. And perhaps Powers's column will encourage others in the mainstream media to subject Planned Parenthood to some much-needed scrutiny.

Read Prof. New's entire column to understand his argument and see the citations.

Here's my observation: Planned Parenthood has put its theory into practice and it has not worked.

Planned Parenthood has been distributing more and more contraception for 40+ years and yet continues to break new records in the number of abortions it performs each year.

What a Woman Should Know About Birth Control

The consequences of birth control clearly demonstrate an unhealthy, anti-culture and anti-life impact that raises major ethical concerns. Use of birth control is like intentionally eating unhealthy, nutrition-less food just for the pleasure of eating. A steady diet will kill you. In much the same way, a steady diet of birth control kills relationships.

Chris Kahlenborn and Ann Moell,
"What a Woman Should Know About Birth Control,"
OneMoreSoul.com, December 17, 2009.

[Despite] receiving more and more money from the federal government every year, Planned Parenthood continues to perform more abortions every year (in fact, the [data seem] more to suggest that more contraception = MORE abortions, for reasons I'll explain below).

So if PP were a company that promised to deliver contraception for the purpose of lowering the abortion rate, would you see [the data] as a sign of success? Of course not!

Contraception and Abortion

Contraception does not bring down the abortion rate in the U.S. for at least 3 simple, intuitive reasons:

1. Contraception fails. Even if contraception worked 99 out of 100 times (it doesn't, not even close), all you need to do is have sex 100 times and, well, there you go. Contraception reduces the possibility of pregnancy in individual cases, not over a lifetime of sexual activity.

2. Contraception creates a culture of risky sex. If people convince themselves there will be no long-term consequences to risky sex, they are more likely to engage in it. And when their contraception fails because they have put themselves in danger of having an "unwanted" pregnancy in the first place, abortions follow next, because abortions are the ultimate "birth control" method.

3. Contraception is already omnipresent in our society. Seriously, who believes anymore that someone who wants contraception cannot find it? Contraception is in our drug stores, gas stations, bathrooms and doctors' offices. It's already everywhere.

And in fact, the statistics would seem to suggest that contraception and abortion are directly related, not inversely related. In other words: *more* contraception encourages more risky sex, which equals *more* need for abortions when contraception inevitably fails.

Planned Parenthood has no answer to these deeper reasons why contraception does not reduce the number of abortions, because when it comes right down to it, Planned Parenthood isn't about preventing pregnancies, it's about *preventing unwanted births.* Birth control therefore comes in two forms in their mind: contraception and abortion. Ideologically, they cannot separate the two.

I find that simple illustrations are sometimes more effective than lengthy posts (even though I've just written one above), so allow me to conclude with this simple illustration:

Planned Parenthood saying more contraception will result in less abortions is like BP saying more deep-water drilling will result in less oil spills.

Feel free to complete this sentence above in a different way with your own comparison. I prefer to use ones that Progressives will have a tough time denying/ignoring.

Bottom line: However we choose to explain it, we all ought to be working on busting the birth-control myth once and for all. My thanks to Kirsten Powers, Michael New and others who have helped get us started. It's up to us to finish and win this argument. Lives depend on it.

> *"When will we Americans face up to the fact that it's better to proactively prevent conception rather than abort a fetus at the back end of that conception?"*

Abortion, Birth Control, Common Sense, and Reality

Frosty Wooldridge

Frosty Wooldridge is an author and a political commentator. In the following viewpoint, he underscores the inanity of denying birth control to women for religious reasons, outlining all the consequences of allowing unchecked population growth around the world. Wooldridge asserts that the best way to lessen the number of abortions worldwide is birth control and family planning. He suggests that those opposed to funding family planning services in the United States and abroad start using their common sense and deal with reality.

As you read, consider the following questions:

1. According to Wooldridge, how many abortions are performed worldwide every year?

2. How many children does Wooldridge say are born in third world countries every year?

3. How much does it cost to fund international family planning, according to the author?

Human beings perform 46 million abortions annually around the planet. Year in and year out! That's 46 million women requesting and accepting an abortion of their fetus. According to the World Health Organization, 96 percent of those abortions represent a secondary form of birth control. That means they did not have access to birth control on the front end. It means they either couldn't feed a child, shelter it or provide for it—or they already had birthed too many children they couldn't feed or care for.

At the same time, eight million adults and ten million children under the age of 12 die of starvation and related diseases annually around this planet—18 million human beings. Year in and year out! In my world bicycle travels, I witnessed such massive human die-offs personally. I also witnessed living conditions that would turn the stomach of an average Canadian, European, American. (Sources: *Time* Magazine, World Health Organization)

Two billion human beings live on less than $2.00 per day and over 1.5 billion human beings cannot procure a clean glass of drinking water. Over 2.1 billion humans do not have access to or use of flush toilets with water sewage treatment plants. In India, 1,000 children under the age of 12 die of dysentery, diarrhea and other waterborne diseases every day of the year. (Source: www.populationmedia.org) Yet, without birth control, India grows by an added 12 million annually, net gain, on their way from 1.2 billion to 1.6 billion in 39 years. The Ganges River, which I witnessed, flows into the ocean loaded with raw sewage, chemicals and cremated human bodies. It forms a 10,000-mile dead zone at its mouth— where few marine creatures can survive the polluted waters. Today!

Another impoverished nation, Haiti, long before the earthquake, suffered under 9.1 million people on a tiny island desecrated by human overload. They cut 98 percent of their trees. Remember Easter Island's human population fiasco? Result: extinction of their civilization! Haitians run billions of gallons of raw sewage into the ocean. They live in utter poverty, and yet, because the Catholic Church curtails any birth control, Haiti, already living in appalling human misery—expects to add another 3.1 million onto that island within another decade or so. Because of the lack of birth control, Haitian women birth thousands of children they cannot feed, care for or house. Illiteracy: almost 100%. Definition and cause of their poverty: illiteracy, religious mandates and babies.

The third world adds 80 million children annually, net gain. Fact: 57 million humans die off around the planet every year. Humans birth 57 million to replace them while birthing another 80 million to create a net gain—on our way to adding 2 to 3 billion more humans within 40 years.

In other words, the human race seems to love its suffering, its deaths by starvation via all religions that stand against birth control and family planning.

Here in the USA, according to Dottie Lamm, *Denver Post* last Sunday [February 15, 2011], "A full 69 percent of African-American children are raised by a single parent, usually the mother."

They birthed those children because they either didn't have money or access to birth control. Cost to U.S. taxpayers in Aid to [Families with] Dependent Children: billions since 1965 when government programs paid for those women to be non-responsible for their actions.

White, Black, Hispanic—no difference! Current food stamp usage: 43 million Americans too uneducated, too poor, or incapable of holding down a job to buy food! (Source: Reuters News)

Current high school dropout rates across the nation: 76 percent in Detroit, Michigan; 50 percent in Denver, Colorado; 55 percent in Los Angeles; and most other major cities. Result: 7,000 teenagers per day drop out of high school, 1 every 26 seconds—total of 1.2 million annually—illiterate teens hitting our streets. (Source: Brian Williams, NBC News, CNN)

We may prefer to ignore these sobering statistics, but they will not ignore us or our civilization—given enough time—complete breakdown of our welfare, educational, medical and prison systems.

The Great Abortion Debate

Last week [February 13–19, 2011], the U.S. House of Representatives voted down funds for international family planning as well as in the United States, i.e., birth control, family counseling regarding "wanted births" as well as termination of pregnancy. They removed the very funds that could alleviate human suffering by providing birth control and family counseling for millions of America's and third world poor.

Let me be clear: I am not in favor of abortion. Used as birth control, it remains insensible! Common sense: I am in favor of birth control so that abortion would become largely obviated.

If the House carries through with its "charge" to stop family planning, sex education and family size counseling—its collective choice will generate added millions to that 46 million annual abortions. At the same time, it will cause millions more starvations of adults and children that do become born. It will add to environmental devastation now taking place around the planet as we add 80 million humans annually.

Consider These Financial Outlays on Top of Human Degradation

Cost of international family planning: $130 million annually. Planned Parenthood in the USA: Less than $50 million.

Cost of the Iraq and Afghanistan wars: $12 billion every 30 days. That's correct; we pay out $12 billion every month to kill people. We killed millions in Korea. We killed over 2.1 million in the Vietnam War. We masterfully snuff out lives in other countries. We have killed hundreds of thousands in Iraq and Afghanistan while displacing 2.5 million as refugees.

I must ask: How many rational people reading this column think it's okay to kill, maim and displace THAT many people in other countries—spend THAT much money on human death—and stand by to witness THAT much misery around the planet, as well as accelerating environmental carnage, while the majority of scientists assure us accelerating backlash by Mother Earth?

You find those actions unconscionable don't you. Yet by refusing to speak out, you remain complicit in denying to support birth control for women that desperately need it in the USA and abroad.

Tell me—and your friends—why you support the pope's advocacy against birth control when you see the poignant results in Haiti, Mexico and every other Catholic-dominated country. The same goes for Islam, Buddhism, Hindus and other religions. What malady within humanity propels human wretchedness over common sense?

When will we Americans face up to the fact that it's better to proactively prevent conception rather than abort a fetus at the back end of that conception? When will we come to our senses and support birth control rather than do everything in our power to stop it—yet stand gasping in anger at the abortion rates?

You're invited to get off your "righteous indignation" and get down to reality. Get down to reasoned thinking! Get down to the nitty-gritty of how fast our civilization fails to deal with reality.

As these children grow into illiteracy, poverty, misery, drugs, ghettoes and welfare—you pay the bills. We're losing the "quality" of our citizens. Every human being wants and deserves to be successful. We need their positive impact on our country, not the other way around. Wouldn't it be better for the House of Representatives to vote in $140 million for birth control for the whole year rather than $12 billion for killing people every 30 days in Iraq and Afghanistan? Discrepancy: $144 billion for war versus $140 million for birth control. What's your choice? When will you speak up?

> "Destroying an embryo, even prior to implantation in the womb, has serious moral implications."

There Are Moral Implications to Taking Emergency Contraception

Lauren Salz

Lauren Salz is a contributor to Columbia Daily Spectator. *In the following viewpoint, she argues that the consequences of taking emergency contraception, which prevents an egg from implanting in a woman's uterus, are similar to those of having an abortion: Both actions result in the destruction of a human life. Salz contends that the moral implications of taking emergency contraception are very serious and require a woman to examine her conscience. She observes that this decision is taken too lightly in our current cultural climate.*

As you read, consider the following questions:

1. According to the website Go Ask Alice!, how long after unprotected sexual intercourse can a woman take emergency contraception?

Lauren Salz, "Think Twice About Plan B," *Columbia Daily Spectator*, March 24, 2009.

2. According to Barnard College Health Services, will emergency contraception work if a woman is already pregnant?

3. According to Salz, what is the difference between taking Plan B and having an abortion?

One night, a student has unprotected sex. Panicked, and worried about pregnancy, she rushes to the pharmacy to get Plan B. Without thinking twice, she takes the emergency "contraceptive." After all, it's not an abortion.

I surveyed my friends to see what they would do in the case of an emergency. "I would take the morning-after pill," was the nearly unanimous response. When they were asked if they would have an abortion in the case of an accidental pregnancy, the general response was, "I don't know. I'd have to think about it."

Clearly, most of these students do not think that Plan B can end a pregnancy. And you can't blame them, considering where their medical information is coming from and the misnomer of emergency "contraception."

Clarifying Plan B

Let's Go Ask Alice!

In a post titled "Morning-after pill," Alice [of Go Ask Alice!, an advice website run by Columbia University] writes:

> "Also known as emergency contraception, the 'morning-after pill' is a high dose of birth control pills taken within 120 hours (or five days) after unprotected intercourse to prevent pregnancy.... Emergency contraception (EC) is not to be confused with RU-486 (mifepristone), a pill that causes medical/chemical abortion in pregnant women within 49 days from the first day of their last menstrual period."

So, there are no moral questions about taking Plan B? It is simply contraception, a way to prevent pregnancy? Not an abortion? From our friend Alice:

"If your friend had unprotected sex within the last few days, she may want to consider the morning-after pill (also called Plan B). . . . The morning-after pill is not an abortion since this pill works to prevent pregnancy from occurring at all."

More Clarification

Let's see if the women's college across the street has any advice. While sitting in the waiting room in Barnard [College] Student Health Services one day, I browsed the publications on the table in front of me. In *Barbelle*, a student-run magazine aiming to "provide the Barnard community with the most current and well-researched information," I found an article titled "The DL on EC." It informed me that "Emergency Contraception does not cause an abortion. . . . Some people think that EC is the same as RU-486. This is incorrect; EC is a contraceptive used to prevent a woman from getting pregnant."

I checked out the official Barnard Emergency Contraception page. I discovered you could even obtain a small advance supply of Plan B from Health Services, and that "if you are already pregnant, emergency contraception will not work."

An FDA Exploration

But what is the mechanism that causes this miracle pill to work? According to the Food and Drug Administration, and the makers of Plan B themselves, not only can Plan B work "like a birth control pill to prevent pregnancy mainly by stopping the release of an egg from the ovary. . . . It is possible that Plan B may also work by preventing fertilization of an egg (the uniting of sperm with the egg) or by preventing attachment (implantation) to the uterus (womb), which usually occurs beginning 7 days after release of an egg from the ovary."

So in short, it is possible that taking Plan B will cause a woman's body to reject an already fertilized egg. That sounds like ending a pregnancy to me.

However, according to the FDA and the maker of Plan B, "Plan B will not do anything to a fertilized egg already attached to the uterus. The pregnancy will continue."

Misleading Information

It seems that their definition of pregnancy is implantation of the embryo onto the uterus. But this is misleading. Destroying an embryo, even prior to implantation in the womb, has serious moral implications.

Prior to conception, a sperm and an egg are part of the parents. A sperm or an egg is missing half of the genetic parts necessary to be an independent member of the *Homo sapiens* species. Once combined, however, the sperm and the egg become a new organism. Unaffected by outside forces such as an abortion or Plan B, a human embryo will likely follow its genetic programming to become a fully functioning adult. Embryos already have the same DNA they will have throughout their entire lives. So Plan B possibly destroys a member of our species that might already have a preference for savory or sweet, have an aptitude for athletics, or enough talent to be the next American Idol.

The consequences of taking Plan B are possibly as dire as the consequences of having an abortion. The difference is that when taking Plan B, a woman doesn't know yet if an embryo has been formed. But the possibilities are the same: the destruction of a vulnerable member of our species for the sake of convenience of a bigger member of our species. An unplanned pregnancy during college certainly has a disruptive effect on a student's life, but it is not life-ending. Please, think twice before you possibly end a life.

> *"Scientific evidence about EC's [emergency contraception's] mechanism of action, supported by consensus within the medical community and numerous federal agencies, consistently indicates that EC does not cause abortion."*

Emergency Contraception Does Not Cause Abortion

Bixby Center for Global Reproductive Health

The Bixby Center for Global Reproductive Health is a center run by the University of California, San Francisco to address domestic and international problems of reproductive health. In the following viewpoint, researchers report that the scientific consensus states that emergency contraception (EC) is not the same as abortion. Unfortunately, the viewpoint asserts, much of the media coverage of the issue presents misleading and inaccurate information, which has real-world policy implications. If policy makers begin to define life as beginning at fertilization instead of implantation, according to the viewpoint, some states will use it to restrict access to contraception. This would be counterproductive, the viewpoint argues, because EC decreases the need for abortions by preventing pregnancy.

As you read, consider the following questions:

1. According to the viewpoint, what percentage of fertilized eggs fail to implant in a woman's uterus?

2. According to an analysis of newspaper coverage of EC between 1992 and 2002, what percentage of articles confused EC and abortion at least once?

3. How many pregnancies in the United States that would have resulted in abortion were prevented by the use of EC in 2000, according to statistics presented in the viewpoint?

The establishment of a pregnancy occurs over several days and involves a series of steps. First, in the process of ovulation, a woman's ovary must release an egg, which remains viable for 12 to 24 hours. Next, sperm, which can remain viable in a woman's reproductive tract for up to 72 hours, must travel to the fallopian tube and penetrate the egg, known as fertilization. Finally, the fertilized egg must be transported to the uterus, where it must implant in the uterine lining. As many as 50 percent of fertilized eggs fail to implant. Implantation occurs approximately six to seven days after fertilization.

Pregnancy begins *after* implantation. This medically accepted definition is endorsed by the American College of Obstetricians and Gynecologists, the U.S. Department of Health and Human Services (HHS), the Food and Drug Administration (FDA), the National Library of Medicine, and the National Institutes of Health. For example, in its *Code of Federal Regulations*, HHS states that, "Pregnancy encompasses the period of time from implantation until delivery." In addition, the FDA follows this definition in its approval process for new contraceptives, including emergency contraception (EC). However, it is important to note that individuals may have varying definitions of when pregnancy begins.

How Does EC Prevent Pregnancy?

The process by which a drug achieves a particular effect on the body is known as its mechanism of action. EC has three possible mechanisms of action, depending on when in a woman's menstrual cycle it is taken. EC may prevent pregnancy by:

1. *Preventing ovulation:* If taken during the first half of the menstrual cycle, EC may prevent the release of the egg from the ovary.

2. *Preventing fertilization:* EC may thicken the cervical mucus, trapping the sperm before it reaches the egg. It may also slow the transport of the sperm and/or the egg in the fallopian tubes and obstruct fertilization.

3. *Preventing implantation:* If fertilization has already occurred, EC may disrupt the transport of the fertilized egg to the uterus or alter the lining of the uterus, averting implantation.

The most recent research suggests that Plan B—the single-hormone (levonorgestrel) method of EC available in the U.S.—works primarily by interfering with ovulation. Animal studies found that Plan B inhibits or delays ovulation; however, if fertilization has occurred, Plan B can no longer prevent pregnancy (i.e., by disrupting implantation). Moreover, a study of Plan B in women found that the drug works by suppressing the hormonal surge necessary for ovulation to occur; thus, it is only effective if taken before ovulation. The study indicates that Plan B's failure rate can be attributed to instances in which it is taken after ovulation, at which point it is no longer effective.

There is less clinical evidence to support the third mechanism of action—prevention of implantation—for Plan B. Studies of combined-hormone (Yuzpe regimen) EC also indicate that inhibiting implantation is unlikely to be the primary mechanism of action.

EC works in the same way as routine methods of hormonal contraception, including birth control pills and the contraceptive injection, implant, patch, and ring. In addition, the contraceptive protections afforded by breastfeeding share the same mechanism of action as EC.

EC Is Not Medication Abortion

EC will not disrupt an established pregnancy. If EC fails to prevent pregnancy, there will be no harm to the woman or the fetus. Pregnancy is only listed as a contraindication to EC because it will not work in this circumstance.

EC is not the same as medication abortion (drug name: mifepristone; brand name: Mifeprex), also known as "the abortion pill" or "RU-486." EC contains progestins—synthetic versions of the hormone progesterone, which is produced by the ovaries and is necessary to establish and support a pregnancy. In contrast, mifepristone is an anti-progestin—it blocks the hormones needed to sustain a pregnancy after implantation. Mifepristone is a safe, effective, nonsurgical method of early abortion. In the U.S., it is used with the drug misoprostol—which causes the uterus to contract and expel its contents—to terminate an established pregnancy up to nine weeks' gestation.

Conflating EC with Abortion Limits Access

Incorrect understanding about EC's mechanism of action is prevalent. A study of EC knowledge found that among women who had heard of EC, nearly one-third mistakenly thought it caused abortion. Inaccurate representations of EC in the mass media compound this problem. An analysis of newspaper coverage of EC between 1992 and 2002 found that nearly half (45 percent) of articles confused EC and abortion at least once. Such confusion can deter women from using EC when needed. In the aforementioned EC knowledge study, women who recognized that EC was not abortion were more than twice as likely to be willing to use it.

Erroneous characterizations of EC's mechanism of action are harmful in the public policy arena because a current movement to define pregnancy as beginning at fertilization makes it easier to conflate EC with abortion. At least 18 states have enacted laws stipulating that pregnancy begins at fertilization, or, more vaguely, at "conception." Similarly, in 2006 South Dakota passed a law banning nearly all abortions in the state, in which it explicitly defined pregnancy as beginning at fertilization. Such definitions could also be used to restrict access to EC and potentially to routine contraceptive methods as well. For example, in its measure to expand Medicaid eligibility for family planning services, Indiana sought to exclude methods "intended to terminate a pregnancy after fertilization."

EC Can Decrease the Need for Abortion

Scientific evidence about EC's mechanism of action, supported by consensus within the medical community and numerous federal agencies, consistently indicates that EC does not cause abortion. To the contrary, EC can *reduce* the need for abortion. One study has estimated that in the U.S., 51,000 pregnancies that would have resulted in abortion were prevented by the use of EC in 2000. It also suggested that 43 percent of the decrease in abortions between 1994 and 2000 (a decline of 110,000) could be attributed to increased use of EC during this period. While half of all pregnancies in the U.S. are unintended, and 42 percent of these end in abortion, only four percent of sexually active women have ever used EC. Ensuring that women have adequate knowledge of and access to EC can increase its use and has the potential to decrease rates of unintended pregnancy and abortion.

> *"Proponents are heralding the approval of ella, which is already available in Europe, as a welcome expansion of women's reproductive options."*

The Drug Ella Is an Important Advance in Emergency Contraception

Sarah Richards

Sarah Richards is a contributor to Slate *magazine. In the following viewpoint, she heralds the release of the new emergency contraception pill known as ella, which can prevent unplanned pregnancy for up to five days after unprotected sex. Richards calls it an important and significant development in the field of emergency contraception. She reports on the controversy surrounding ella, citing critics who have expressed concerns about what they view as the lack of research on the drug.*

As you read, consider the following questions:

1. According to the author, how much does ella reduce the risk of a woman becoming pregnant when taken during the five-day window following intercourse?

2. What is ella's failure rate, according to the viewpoint?

3. What side effects has Watson Pharmaceuticals reported so far from its testing of ella?

Late last week [in August 2010], the Food and Drug Administration announced the approval of a controversial new prescription pill that can prevent unplanned pregnancy for up to five days after unprotected sex. Marketed under the name "ella," the drug is a significant development in the world of so-called "morning-after" pills that aim to thwart ovulation in case sexual assault, broken condoms, or simply bad judgment coincides with the time a woman's body is scheduled to send an egg down the fallopian tubes to be fertilized. Studies have found it to last longer and be twice as effective as Plan B, the version currently on the market, which is only effective for up to 72 hours after intercourse.

What Is Ella?

Proponents are heralding the approval of ella, which is already available in Europe, as a welcome expansion of women's reproductive options. Known as ulipristal acetate, it's chemically similar to the abortion drug RU-486 but will be dispensed in much smaller doses and labeled as an emergency contraceptive. Critics, however, warn that it's a potentially dangerous drug that was inadequately studied. It also reignites the debate about what defines contraception and abortion.

When taken during the five-day window following intercourse, ella is estimated to reduce the risk of becoming pregnant by about two-thirds. In several studies, only 2 percent of women taking ella up to 120 hours after intercourse became pregnant, whereas researchers estimated that at least 5 percent of women not taking the pill would have become pregnant. Ella works through a progesterone blocker that delays the surge of hormones that signal the body it's time to release a mature egg. The main advantage is that a woman can take it

Approving Ella

An FDA [US Food and Drug Administration] Advisory Committee for Reproductive Health Drugs discussed ella in June 2010. The committee unanimously voted that the application for ella provided compelling data on efficacy and sufficient information on safety for the proposed indication of emergency contraception.

The safety and efficacy of ella were demonstrated in two phase III clinical trials. One study was a prospective, multicenter, open-label, single-arm trial conducted in the United States; the other was a randomized, multicenter, single-blind, comparator-controlled trial conducted in the United States, United Kingdom and Ireland.

"FDA Approves Ella Tablets for
Prescription Emergency Contraception,"
US Food and Drug Administration,
August 13, 2010.

while she's ovulating, whereas Plan B has to be taken before the surge begins—approximately 36 hours prior to ovulation—and becomes less effective the longer a woman waits to take it. Since women tend to have higher sex drives right before they ovulate and are more likely to engage in sexual intercourse, being able to take ella closer to an "oops" moment is an important benefit, explains David Archer, professor of obstetrics and gynecology as Eastern Virginia Medical School, who serves as an expert for ella's manufacturer, HRA Pharma of Paris.

Concerns About Ella

But what happens if a woman has already ovulated and her egg has been fertilized before she takes ella? In a normal pregnancy, an embryo takes up to one week from conception to burrow its way into a woman's uterine lining. After the embryo is successfully implanted, a woman is considered to be pregnant, according to the medical definition. Pro-life supporters, who regard the moment when the sperm meets the egg as the beginning of life, are worried about the effect of ella on an embryo before it implants and raised similar concerns following the approval of Plan B in 1999.

At least one study of ella has noted that the drug given at high or repeated doses could alter the lining of a woman's uterus and theoretically impair an embryo's implantation. Archer says there's no evidence that ella can interrupt an existing pregnancy or prevent implantation, and other experts point to the drug's 2 percent failure rate as proof. "At that point, it's just a microscopic ball of about 256 to 550 or 600 cells that will differentiate in the future," explains Archer. "You won't see a head or fingers or any fetal organs."

Critics are also concerned about the lack of research about how ella might affect the development of an embryo of a woman who didn't know she was already pregnant when she took the drug. "RU-486 acts in the body in the same way [that ella does] and can abort a pregnancy," says Donna Harrison, president of the American Association of Pro-life Obstetricians and Gynecologists. "This drug has not been tested in pregnant women. We know that two out of 100 women who take ella will become pregnant. That's two babies who will be exposed to this toxic drug. It's completely unethical." Dr. James Trussell, director of the Office of Population Research at Princeton, who also was a consultant for ella's manufacturer, pointed out that the handful of women who were discovered to be pregnant after taking ella didn't appear to suffer from ill effects. He adds that a woman would have to take "many, many, many times" the amount of the drug to induce an abortion. "And where is someone going to get it?"

More Research Is Needed

Watson Pharmaceuticals will market ella domestically and plans to make it available in late fall. So far, it appears to be safe, and the 4,500 women involved in the studies have only reported minor side effects, including headaches, nausea, and abdominal pain. In the meantime, it needs to be studied further. The drug is an important advance that will undoubtedly be embraced by women who are grateful it can reverse the consequences of regrettable acts and unfortunate contraceptive malfunctions. They will also appreciate the extra days to contact their doctors to secure a prescription.

> *"There is good reason to believe [ella] can also act as an 'abortion drug' in the vein of RU-486, interfering with and indeed ending* implanted *pregnancies."*

The Drug Ella Causes Abortions

Michael Fragoso

Michael Fragoso is a law student and a former policy analyst at the Family Research Council. In the following viewpoint, he contends that ella not only prevents ovulation and embryonic implantation but also can be used to terminate implanted pregnancies. Therefore, it can be classified as an abortion drug. Fragoso is concerned that although ella has been approved by the US Food and Drug Administration (FDA) as emergency contraception, physicians prescribe it for women in the earliest stages of pregnancy. He also charges that federal funds may be used to subsidize it—in effect, the government would be subsidizing an abortifacient, a drug that causes abortion.

As you read, consider the following questions:

1. What has the Drudge Report nicknamed ella, according to Fragoso?

2. What does an SPRM (selective progesterone receptor modulator) do, according to the author?

3. According to Fragoso, what should President [Barack] Obama do about ella immediately?

O n August 13th [2010], the Food and Drug Administration (FDA) approved the drug "ella" (ulipristal acetate) for prescription use as emergency contraception (EC). The agency recommended it for "occasional" use up to five days following either unprotected intercourse or contraceptive failure, causing the Drudge Report to name it the "week-after pill." The innocently named ella has the potential to do far more than merely prevent ovulation or even prevent embryonic implantation: There is good reason to believe it can also act as an "abortion drug" in the vein of [abortion drug] RU-486, interfering with and indeed ending *implanted* pregnancies. As such, the approval of ella rightly ought to have involved more than antiseptic scientific data, institutional reviews, and clinical trials: ella's approval and use raises fundamental questions of life, death, and ethics that our regulatory system is ill-equipped to answer.

The Ella Controversy

Given the probable usefulness of ella as an abortion pill, the FDA's approval of the drug for EC prescription is only the beginning of the controversy surrounding ulipristal. A newly approved abortion drug for EC purposes will warrant future regulatory battles over the drug's labeling, disputes over abortion funding, and, ultimately, demonstrate the inadequacy of our current pharmaceutical regulatory regime in controlling the "off-label" use of drugs. ("Off-label" use of drugs, of course, refers to the use of drugs for purposes outside of their FDA marketing approval. The possibilities for the "off-label" use of ella are obvious.)

News reports on the approval of ella note that it is an improvement over the previous form of emergency contraception "Plan B" (levonorgestrel), which purports to work only seventy-two hours after unprotected sex or contraceptive failure. Levonorgestrel has been used in hormonal contraceptives for decades, and Plan B simply uses a large dose of it to prevent pregnancy by preventing a woman's ovulation. (Plan B's label, however, also notes that it can work by obstructing fertilization of the ovum or by preventing the fertilized embryo from implanting in the womb.) The ulipristal in ella works in a similar manner according to its label: "When taken immediately before ovulation is to occur, ella postpones follicular rupture. The likely primary mechanism of action of ulipristal acetate for emergency contraception is therefore inhibition or delay of ovulation; however, alterations to the endometrium that may affect implantation may also contribute to efficacy." While the operation of the drugs as EC might be similar, ella can boast that it is approved for use up to two days longer than Plan B.

Ella Has the Potential to Cause Abortion

In all likelihood, however, ulipristal does more than simply prevent ovulation or implantation like levonorgestrel. As the American Association of Pro-Life Obstetricians and Gynecologists (AAPLOG) pointed out in their submission to the FDA prior to ella's approval, ulipristal acts as a "selective progesterone receptor modulator" (SPRM). An SPRM acts to block receptors of the hormone progesterone throughout the body. AAPLOG described three ways this could possibly kill the developing child:

> 1. Ulipristal blocks progesterone at the level of the endometrial glands, and destroys the receptivity of the endometrium so that the embryo cannot implant;

2. Ulipristal destroys the capacity of the corpus luteum granulosa cells to produce progesterone; production of progesterone at the corpus luteum level supports the implanted embryo throughout the first 10 weeks of pregnancy; absent this corpus luteal progesterone production, the placenta which feeds the embryo will die; this mechanism of action is identical to the action of RU-486 on the corpus luteum;

3. Ulipristal directly blocks progesterone receptors in the endometrial stromal tissue, identical to the mechanism of action of mifepristone (RU-486) which kills the implanted embryo by directly destroying the maternal component of the placenta.

AAPLOG notes that the second and third abortifacient mechanisms, similar to those of mifepristone, distinguish ulipristal from levonorgestrel, which does not interfere with an implanted embryo. So while ella has been approved for marketing as contraception in the same vein as Plan B, it has the capacity to operate like the (more tightly regulated and more controversial) abortion pill RU-486.

A Useless Label

AAPLOG, in its submission to the FDA, suggested that ella should have a "black box" warning on its label about its abortifacient properties, not unlike the drug Cytotec (misoprostol)—a drug approved for the treatment of certain ulcers that also moonlights as the abortion drug of choice in places where RU-486 is not available. As it stands, the ella label does note that "use of ella is contraindicated during an existing or suspected pregnancy." This notice to users, however, is practically meaningless in the world of drug regulation, as the approved use of a drug by the FDA has more to do with marketing than with use.

FDA approval is a notoriously costly and laborious process, and when a drug company submits a "new drug applica-

Ella Is a Killer

Perhaps ella's most dangerous side effect is the psychological one. It's what ella—and Plan B and RU-486—does to our perception of abortion and human life that is the most deadly.

It's murder at the micro-level, hidden from view and carried out in private. No evidence of the crime; no evidence the child was ever here. Before long abortion at home becomes commonplace. Just pop a pill and eliminate your baby, not unlike getting rid of a headache.

Jennifer Hartline, "A Killer Named Ella:
FDA Approves New Embryocidal Drug," Catholic Online,
August 17, 2010. www.catholic.org.

tion," the drug undergoes no fewer than three phases of clinical testing for a specific population (e.g., "adults"), with specific administration criteria (e.g., "by prescription") for a specific condition (e.g., the treatment of NSAID [nonsteroidal anti-inflammatory drug]-induced gastric ulcers). When the FDA approves a drug, it can be *marketed* by the drug company under the conditions set forth—so the manufacturer can market misoprostol *to adults* to take the drug *by prescription* to treat NSAID ulcers. This marketing takes the form of marketing to "learned intermediaries" (physicians) who then recommend and prescribe the drug to patients, or, more recently "direct to consumer" (DTC) marketing, alerting consumers directly what their options are so they inquire with their physicians about the possibility of taking a drug. (The myriad commercials ending with, "Ask your physician if [drug X] is right for you," following a comically long list of horrible side effects are examples of DTC marketing.) The FDA approval process bears directly on how drug companies can market drugs, not on how physicians can prescribe them.

It is an established fact of law that the FDA does not regulate the practice of medicine. As such, physicians are free to prescribe drugs *as the practice of medicine dictates*, not as the FDA has approved them. This "off-label" prescription of drugs is so commonplace that in some specialties a physician's failure to prescribe a drug in an "unapproved" manner can open her up to malpractice liability. In many ways, this makes sense: In fields such as oncology, time is of the essence in treatment, so the cutting edge of the specialty might rely on accumulated knowledge and academic studies in lieu of plodding regulatory approval in Washington; in pediatrics, most drugs are approved already for adult populations, but getting them approved with a supplemental new drug application for children would be prohibitively costly (leaving aside the ethical problems with conducting clinical trials on children). Thus the current FDA regulatory framework does not constrain "unapproved" uses of drugs.

In the case of ella, this means that its labeled contraindication for pregnant women is wholly irrelevant to how it can be prescribed. While the label professes agnosticism as to how ulipristal might interact with an implanted pregnancy, the science of SPRMs [selective progesterone receptor modulators] like mifepristone is well established. A physician who is aware of ulipristal's embryocidal properties has nothing to prevent him from prescribing ella to a patient in the early stages of pregnancy, regardless of what the FDA label indicates. Indeed, the main constraint on a physician doing so would be the fear of malpractice liability in the case of an adverse event.

Marketing vs. Application

In a sense, ella's manufacturers do not need the FDA to approve ulipristal for anything more than EC. If they were to get it approved as an abortion drug, that would simply allow them to market it as such, and the political and commercial realities of contemporary America make DTC (or even learned intermediary) marketing of an abortion drug a dubious goal for a corporation. With or without FDA approval, the sorts of physicians who prescribe abortion drugs will be able to prescribe ulipristal to terminate a pregnancy.

Herein lies an immediate problem: If ella is labeled for use as emergency contraception, but can be prescribed to effect an abortion, what is to prevent federal monies from subsidizing it as contraception, only to have it used as an abortifacient? Congressman Chris Smith has concluded that coverage of the drug is probably mandated under the recent health care reform act, and has called on President [Barack] Obama to issue an executive order clarifying that federal agencies and affected insurance plans are not to fund the drug. Given the already blurry line between contraceptive family planning and abortion, executive clarification is certainly in order.

Coming Soon: Ella over the Counter

Another development that is probably pending is a dispute over ella's administration criteria. As it stands, it is only available by prescription, in stark contrast to the other available EC, Plan B. When the FDA allowed Plan B to be distributed to adult women without a prescription for over-the-counter distribution for women 18 and older it was hailed by Planned Parenthood's Cecile Richards as "great news for women and great news for women's health." It is highly unlikely that the reproductive health left will be content with the administration discrepancy between the two drugs, and similarly unlikely that Watson will pass up the opportunity to increase the drug's market share as EC by removing the necessity of having a doctor write the prescription (regardless of its capacity to function as an abortion pill). In the coming months and years we should expect a supplemental new drug application from Watson asking for a dual administration label like Plan B, thus allowing adult women to buy ella without prescription. This would put the FDA in the position of approving an OTC abortion pill.

According to Kirsten Moore of the Reproductive Health Technologies Project, ella's approval "was consistent with standard FDA procedure and based on scientific evidence, not politics." Those standard FDA procedures, however, are not well equipped to respond to the unique problems posed by the emergency contraception ulipristal: namely its potential for off-label use as an abortion pill. Even if the FDA were to rightly adopt stricter labeling guidelines warning of abortifacient potential, like those employed with misoprostol, that would only serve to inform consumers, and not have any bearing on physicians who prescribe the drug to perform an abortion. Such warnings will also have little effect on women who purchase the drug on their own, should ella become over-the-counter like its predecessor Plan B, with the intent of procuring an abortion.

Blurring the Line

The possibilities of public funding for ella, its switch to over-the-counter availability, and its usefulness as an abortion drug implicate more than just "scientific evidence," and necessarily involve politics. Drugs like ulipristal further blur the line between contraception and abortion, and lawmakers like Congressman Smith are right to demand that those lines remain bright when it comes to appropriations, regardless of the confusion caused by FDA labeling. More generally, the relatively quiet approval of an abortion drug as contraception should cause us all to step back and consider whether our current regulatory framework is in the best interests not only of Big Pharma, physicians, and patients, but also those of the body politic.

Periodical and Internet Sources Bibliography

The following articles have been selected to supplement the diverse views presented in this chapter.

Lindsay Beyerstein	"Of Course Birth Control Prevents Abortions: Debunking Kirsten Powers," *Big Think*, March 4, 2011. http://bigthink.com.
The Economist	"Abortion and Birth Control: Crazy Sexy Stupid," January 5, 2011.
Kelly Lorenz	"Ella, the 2nd Emergency Birth Control Is on Her Way," Examiner.com, August 25, 2010.
Jeanne Monahan	"Ella and Abortion," *National Review Online*, October 5, 2010. www.nationalreview.com.
Michael New	"Planned Parenthood Under the Microscope: In Defense of Kirsten Powers," *National Review Online*, March 9, 2011. www.nationalreview.com.
Nancy Frazier O'Brien	"Ella's Effects Go Beyond Contraception to Abortion, Experts Say," *Catholic Sun*, August 25, 2011.
Thomas Peters	"Logic 101: Why 'We Need More Birth Control'='We Need More Abortions,'" CatholicVote.org, 2011.
Kirsten Powers	"Busting the Birth-Control Myth," *Daily Beast*, March 4, 2011. www.thedailybeast.com.
Bonnie Rochman	"To Slash the Abortion Rate, Dole Out Birth-Control Pills a Year at a Time," *Time*, February 25, 2011.

OPPOSING
VIEWPOINTS®
SERIES

CHAPTER 2

What Impact Does the Birth Control Pill Have on Society?

Chapter Preface

For years, there has been a rising anticipation for a male oral contraceptive, also known as a male birth control pill. With nearly eleven million American women on the birth control pill, many birth control advocates wonder when men will finally have the option to take a male oral contraceptive. One of the reasons it has taken so long to develop is the unique challenges the male reproductive system poses for researchers and scientists. After all, a man releases between 250 to 300 million sperm in each ejaculation. How can a male birth control pill stop all of those sperm from reaching a woman's egg?

Initially, researchers modeled the male birth control pill on the female version, which uses a hormone-based approach to preventing pregnancy. In a male, sperm is produced when a fertility hormone in the pituitary gland, ICSH, signals the testes to produce sperm. When the cycle of sperm production is complete, the testes release testosterone and a hormone called inhibin, which messages the brain that there is enough sperm. Researchers determined that since testosterone was one of the hormones that turned off sperm production, keeping a man's level of testosterone at a consistently high level would ensure no further sperm production.

However, keeping the male testosterone level elevated led to some rather disturbing side effects, including abnormal liver function and enlargement of the prostate. To counter these side effects, researchers introduced the hormone progestogen, which is found in female birth control pills. Researchers found that regular injections of progestogen counteracted the side effects for a large majority of the men tested. Researchers were left with the question: What man would want to go through all of that when a condom would solve the problem and not require all those hormones?

Researchers turned from turning off the production of sperm to disarming them. One idea that emerged in 2005 from a research team at the University of Massachusetts was that by blocking a certain protein that enables a sperm's tail, sperm would be produced but unable to swim to a woman's egg. In 2011 at Columbia University, a researcher discovered another potential method. A certain compound, BMS-189453, prevents the body from breaking down vitamin A, which is essential in sperm production. In practice, this compound renders men temporarily infertile. Researchers are concerned about the side effects of this compound, and further testing needs to be completed.

Considered the most promising idea for male birth control, reversible inhibition of sperm under guidance (RISUG) was developed thirty years ago by an Indian scientist, Sujoy Guha, but has just started to receive widespread media attention in the United States. RISUG involves a one-time injection of a gel, known as Vasalgel, which damages and basically incapacitates sperm as they are being ejaculated. Birth control advocates are excited by the results of testing in India that shows that it is very effective at protecting against unplanned pregnancies and has no serious side effects.

Although research on male birth control methods continues and has produced some promising results, there are many people who wonder how men will respond to the availability of a male birth control pill. This is one issue explored in the following chapter, which examines the impact the birth control pill has on society. Other topics include the pill's environmental consequences, its affect on sexual activity, and the question of whether it has benefited or hurt society.

> "This denigration of the pill's importance is the worst sort of historical revisionism, based not only on a distrust of the male medical establishment . . . but on a general antagonism to science itself that is part of the unreason pervading American culture today."

The Birth Control Pill Benefits Women

Susan Jacoby

Susan Jacoby is an author and the program director at the Center for Inquiry. In the following viewpoint, she offers an appreciation of the birth control pill on its fiftieth anniversary. Jacoby criticizes recent attacks on the birth control pill by renowned feminists like Gloria Steinem, arguing that without the pill many women would not have been able to take advantage of the economic and education opportunities opened up by feminism in the 1970s. She points out that the birth control pill was a method financed and supported by women who wanted to assert more control over their reproductive lives and has been a major boon to women of all classes throughout the years.

As you read, consider the following questions:

1. Who coined the term "birth control," according to Jacoby?

2. Who does the author say financed the initial research on the birth control pill?

3. What does the author cite as the pregnancy risk of the birth control pill if used correctly?

On May 9, 1960, the Food and Drug Administration [FDA] approved the marketing of the first birth control pill in the United States. As far as I am concerned, nothing in my lifetime has done more to empower women and improve their lives. There would have been a feminist movement without the pill, but lacking the ability to control their fertility—with or without the consent of men—many fewer women would have been poised to take advantage of the economic and educational opportunities opened up by feminism in the 1970s. Yet Gloria Steinem tells *Time* magazine that the importance of the pill is "overrated." In the *Huffington Post*, Dr. Christiane Northrup—one of those New Agey MDs who has made a fortune emphasizing holistic healing over science-based medicine—writes that the pill "fits well with society's view of the female body as something that requires outside control." Perhaps Northrup possesses some magic formula by which sexually active women can click their heels three times to limit the number of their children.

This denigration of the pill's importance is the worst sort of historical revisionism, based not only on a distrust of the male medical establishment that was a strong and well-founded strain in feminism in the 1960s and 1970s but on a general antagonism to science itself that is part of the unreason pervading American culture today. For feminist leaders like Steinem, the idea that the importance of the pill has been exaggerated may simply be a matter of ego, of a reluctance to acknowledge that feminism, like so many successful social movements, was the product of many forces converging simultaneously.

The Experiences of a Young Woman in the 1960s

Let me tell you how it was. I was 15 when the FDA approved the pill, and I was the product of a time and a community in which nice girls didn't have (or at least they didn't admit to actually having) sex. In my junior year of high school, a girl I knew quite well became pregnant, and there was a huge fight over whether she would be allowed to stay in school after her pregnancy became visible. Surprisingly (most pregnant girls at this time were simply expelled), she was permitted to finish her senior year. In fact, there could have been no scarier anti-sex lesson than the sight of this girl, hardly able to fit behind her desk, removed entirely from the anything resembling normal teenage life. I never discussed my real views on sex, any more than I talked about my atheism, but I read all about the pill and promised myself that when I met someone with whom I wanted to begin my life as a sexual woman, I would somehow manage to obtain a prescription for the pill.

It wasn't easy. When I entered college in 1963, 18-year-olds were still minors, and birth control was theoretically obtainable only if you could show that you were married. Even Planned Parenthood did not dispense contraceptives to unmarried women. It was only in 1965, in *Griswold v. Connecticut*, that the Supreme Court established a right to privacy allowing the distribution of contraceptives to married couples—a right that was not routinely extended to the unmarried for some years. Nevertheless, the pill—which could be prescribed for "menstrual irregularity"—already gave many doctors cover for bending the old rules. In 1964, I concocted a story about being engaged and wanting to start the pill so that my cycles would be regular by the time of my wedding. It was humiliating to tell this lie, and I am quite certain that the doctor did not believe me, but he wrote me a prescription anyway.

I wanted to become a newspaper reporter, and I was already working for a professional paper while going to school. I knew that a pregnancy would be the end of my ambitions. I'd already seen it, as more than one girl dropped out during her freshman year because she "had to get married." I also knew girls who had gone through the terrible, life-altering experience of being sent to a home for unwed mothers and giving up their babies for adoption. And one girl in my dormitory bled to death from an illegal abortion. Then there was the amount of emotional energy wasted by young women checking every hour to see whether they had gotten their period.

The Female Responsibility

You may say, as the religious right does today, that celibacy is the way to deal with pregnancy anxiety. I say, as a woman and a secularist, that saying yes or no to sex—without having to "pay" by risking the rest of one's life—is a basic human right. And it is harder for women to exercise that right. With the exception of a committed couple in a long-term, monogamous relationship, there is no situation in which a man has as great a stake in preventing an unwanted pregnancy as a woman. This is not a criticism of men but a biological fact: Pregnancy and childbirth happen within a woman's body.

The battle over birth control—a term coined by Margaret Sanger in the early 20th century—was being waged long before there were effective means of artificial contraception. In 1873, Congress passed a law defining information about contraception as obscenity and banning its distribution through the mail. State and local "Comstock laws," named after the anti-vice crusader Anthony Comstock, remained on the books until the 1960s—as the Roman Catholic Church took over the anti–birth control crusade from reactionary Protestants in the 20th century. Birth control was always a secularist cause: Before World War I, only freethinkers and socialists unequivocally condemned the Comstock law definitions of birth control information as obscene. Robert Green Ingersoll, the "Great Agnostic," was one of the first public figures of either sex to link birth control with the independence of women. Speaking in 1899, Ingersoll envisioned the day when science would "make women the owner, the mistress of herself" by enabling her "to decide for herself whether she will or will not become a mother."

That promise was realized by the pill, which was the result of a collaboration between physiology researcher Gregory Pincus and Dr. John Rock, a Catholic who was trying to develop a hormonal method to help infertile women conceive. In one of the many unintended consequences in the history of science, Rock discovered that a hormone-based pill could also be used to prevent conception by suppressing ovulation. The research was financed initially by Katharine Dexter McCormick, a longtime friend of Margaret Sanger and wife of the heir to the International Harvester fortune. Sanger, who was born in 1879 and watched her Catholic mother die after 18 pregnancies, had a lifelong dream of a contraceptive that women would be able to use to limit their fertility without the cooperation or even the knowledge of men. She dreamed of a world in which a woman's fate would not be determined by a husband who did not care whether he made her pregnant 18 times. That dream was realized, for millions of women around the world in societies with widely varying attitudes toward women's rights, with the development of the pill.

Thus, the pill was hardly a male plot to "control" women's bodies; it was the culmination of a long research effort, financed at the outset by a woman and carried out by two men who wanted women to have more, not less, power over their reproductive lives. Dr. Rock had even hoped that the pill, be-

The Pervasive Influence of the Birth Control Pill

It became a symbol of women's rights and generational change—and, for a time, the focus of a debate over whether it led to declining morals.

The pill was groundbreaking in other ways: Women today have a wide range of effective contraceptive choices, virtually all of them variations on the pill. Concerns about adverse effects linked to the early, high-dose oral contraceptives galvanized feminists and gave rise to the consumer health movement. Americans no longer assume doctors, regulators and drug companies know what's best for them.

Rita Rubin, "The Pill:
50 Years of Birth Control Changed Women's Lives,"
USA Today, *May 8, 2010.*

cause it works by manipulating a woman's hormonal system, would be approved by the Catholic Church, which forbade older barrier methods of birth control. In this he was disappointed, but Catholic women used the pill in huge numbers anyway.

New Challenges

The Christian Right is still trying to block unmarried women's access to contraceptives (though its representatives don't campaign against selling condoms in drugstores), and it has also played a huge role in limiting teenagers' access to birth control information. But that does not explain the disparagement of the pill's importance by veterans of the feminist movement, who ought to be celebrating the anniversary of this scientific advance as one of the keys to women's liberation in our time.

Part of the explanation is the mush purveyed by people like Northrup. She writes, "Other methods, for example diaphragms, condoms and fertility awareness, have been actively downplayed even though, when used properly, they are nearly as effective as the pill." This is simply not true, according to Planned Parenthood, which keeps the best statistics on all forms of birth control.

In case you don't know what "fertility awareness" means, it's another name for the rhythm method, aka Vatican roulette—being aware of the timing of your menstrual cycles and avoiding sex around the time of ovulation. According to Planned Parenthood, "fertility awareness" is the least effective of all methods of contraception—if it can be called contraception at all. The lowest pregnancy rate (for couples who have the greatest success with this dubious method) is 12 unplanned pregnancies per 100 women each year. The more likely rate is 25 per 100—not very good odds for a young woman trying to plan her future. The diaphragm's rate of unplanned pregnancies is 6 to 16 percent—again, ranging from the most consistent use to average use.

The Pill as Birth Control

The pill, however, has a pregnancy risk of only 1 percent risk if used correctly, rising to 8 percent if used incorrectly. The condom actually does have almost as low a rate as the pill, if used correctly every time—2 percent—but that figure rises to 15 percent if used incorrectly. In truth, the effectiveness of all birth control methods is best measured by assuming that everyone slips up once in a while. So the rate of unplanned pregnancy, which is only 8 percent per year even if a woman does forget a pill once in a while, is nearly double that for the condom and diaphragm, and more than three times higher for the so-called "natural" rhythm method. And, above all, the pill is entirely under a woman's control. How, pray tell, can any woman ensure that a man will use a condom with utmost care? (The *Huffington Post*'s publication of Northrup's assertions about the comparative effectiveness of various birth control methods, without vetting them with standard medical sources, provides an excellent illustration of the inadequacies of fact-checking on Internet news sites.)

Male and female sterilization (which are, by the way, the most popular forms of contraception among married couples who already have all the children they want) are also 99 percent effective—but they are obviously inappropriate for young women. The pill is the only reversible method of birth control that, when used properly, provides near-certain protection.

Early Criticisms

The pill is not perfect. Much of the early feminist opposition, stated most forcefully in 1969 by Barbara Seaman in *The Doctors' Case Against the Pill* (reissued and updated in the 1990s) rested on the fact that it had not been extensively tested and represented an unprecedented experiment involving the use of a drug by a huge, healthy population. It is true that the pill had been tested on fewer than 900 women in Puerto Rico when it was approved by the FDA in 1960. (At the time, most states had laws against testing any drug to be used for contraceptive purposes.) And it is also true that the first pill had many more short-term side effects than later, lower-dose pills. Moreover, it is still true that the pill should not be used by women who smoke, because it increases the risk of stroke. (Of course, these women would be a lot better off if they would just quit smoking.)

But Seaman, who died in 2008 and was a friend of mine, never took into account the vital risk-benefit equation that applied even in the pill's early years: It did represent an unknown risk, but the unknown risk was being taken for a huge and certain benefit. Moreover, time has proved that the pill is safe for most healthy young women. A 40-year study of 46,000 women, conducted by the Royal College of General Practitioners found that women who had taken birth control pills have a longer life expectancy and are less likely to have died from any cause than women who have never taken the pill. This study is not the final word, as it cannot analyze long-term effects on younger women who have used later versions of the pill. But there is nothing in this study to bear out the early fears that the pill would have long-term, severely adverse effects on women's health. Nor can this study ever measure what the impact of the hundreds of thousands of unwanted pregnancies would have been had these women not used the pill.

The Pill and Sexually Transmitted Diseases

The pill also does not offer any protection against sexually transmitted diseases ([STDs] a subject that neither doctors nor the public knew much about in the 1960s). But neither does any other method of contraception except condoms. And one thing is certain: A man who doesn't care enough to use a condom in order to protect his partner and himself from pregnancy certainly won't do it to guard against STDs.

In any event, I simply do not agree with anyone who does not see the pill as a major boon to women. Opposition to birth control—particularly to woman-controlled contraception—was always based on the idea that without fear of pregnancy, all sexual prohibitions would collapse. This attitude was well embodied by a 1966 cover story in *U.S. News & World Report* that asked ominously, "Can its [the pill's] availability to all women of childbearing age lead to sexual anarchy?" The word "promiscuity" was used constantly in all of these hand-wringing critiques of the pill, and the premise—a very revealing one about the double standard—was that women were the guardians of chastity and they would stop acting in that role once they no longer risked unwanted pregnancy.

I have no doubt that the pill dealt a death blow to the idea that all women should be virgins on their wedding night (an idea that never, of course, reflected reality). But there is a huge difference between promiscuity—which implies indiscriminate sex—and having a number of selected sexual partners before marriage.

Gloria Steinem has a short memory if she thinks that the significance of the pill has been overrated. When I was young, one of the most common excuses used by employers who refused to train women for high-level jobs—and by professional schools with a tiny female quota—was that women would just get pregnant at an early age and the investment would be wasted. Indeed, when I applied for a job at the *Washington Post* at age 19, I was asked by the director of personnel to sit down and write an essay about how I would combine motherhood with a career (a subject on which every 19-year-old is surely an expert). The new antidiscrimination laws championed by the women's movement during the 1970s played a huge role in ending these practices, but so did the growing realization of employers that all young women, thanks to the pill, were delaying childbirth and were having fewer children altogether.

So thank you, Margaret Sanger, Katharine McCormick, Gregory Pincus, and John Rock.

I am convinced that the fruit of your dreams, your money and your science did more good for more people than any other invention of the 20th century. And it does not in any way underrate the importance of 1970s feminism to say that we might not have been able to achieve what we did if you had not achieved what you did.

"The sex drive is largely physiological: When women change their sexual physiology it should be expected that their sex drive will change."

The Birth Control Pill Has Led to a Decline in Sexual Activity

Janet E. Smith

Janet E. Smith is an instructor at the Sacred Heart Major Seminary in Detroit, Michigan. In the following viewpoint, she observes that women's libidos are declining to the point where pharmaceutical companies are testing a form of Viagra for women. Smith attributes the decline of the female libido to the use of the birth control pill, arguing that chemicals in the pill block the production of testosterone and demolish the female sex drive. She recommends that women interested in a healthy, vibrant sex life stop using chemical contraceptives and utilize the Natural Family Planning method of birth control.

As you read, consider the following questions:

1. What does the work of Dr. Helen Fisher show about women taking chemical contraceptives, according to Smith?

2. How does the author believe contraception undermines the sexual experience?

3. According to Smith, how effective is Natural Family Planning as a method of contraception?

This year [2010] there was a predictable amount of hoopla surrounding the 50th anniversary of "the pill." Many pundits told us that the pill had delivered as promised: Women had become liberated. Sex in the city! Sex in dorm rooms! Sex behind bleachers! Women have it all.

But wait. Now comes word that women aren't all that interested in sex anymore. Their libidos are waning to the point that pharmaceutical companies are racing to find a Pink Viagra: a new pill; a pill that will restore the desire to have the sex that the pill made possible.

Why don't women want to have sex? Is it because they are so absorbed in their careers? Is it because these careers force women to sacrifice their femininity and males to sacrifice their masculinity and thus the vivifying difference between males and females no longer exists? Why do women need males? Women have everything males have; they can do everything males do; what do males have to offer?

Certainly the above explanations are not unlikely and almost certainly have a degree of truth but—still—can the desire of female for male be so easily obliterated? Isn't the attraction even more elemental than caps and chaps and buttons and bows?

The Role of the Pill

I find it strange that commentators have not identified a very likely cause of the lack of female libido. The pill, indeed all chemical contraceptives, has as a common side effect, a reduced sex drive. It is well documented both scientifically and anecdotally that the hormones in chemical contraceptives prevent a woman from producing the level of testosterone needed for her to have a healthy sex drive. The sex drive is largely physiological: When women change their sexual physiology it should be expected that their sex drive will change. Many of the chemical contraceptives put a woman's body into a state of pseudo pregnancy. Researchers discovered that pregnant women don't ovulate (and women who don't ovulate cannot get pregnant), so they learned how to deceive the female body into "thinking" it is pregnant so it wouldn't ovulate. Nature also establishes that women who are pregnant generally do not have strong sex drives; it serves no evolutionary benefit.

Studies on the effects of hormones on male/female relationships have been proliferating. The work of Dr. Helen Fisher, among others, shows that women who use chemical contraceptives prefer more feminine looking men or "safer" men; when they stop using chemical contraceptives, they discover they have a higher sex drive but are not much interested in the male they chose when they were using the chemical contraceptives. Males are also much more attracted sexually to women who have fertile cycles; they produce more testosterone when around women who are fertile. Certainly the ardor of the male partner affects the female response.

Sex as an Obligation

A friend of mine once told me how her seven brothers and sisters one day had a frank and open discussion of their sex lives. Six couples, double income, no kids, lamented the lack of sex in their marriages; the females, attractive, well dressed and well employed, confessed they felt sex was just one more chore demanded of them at the end of a long day. The males, equally attractive, well dressed and well employed, stated they felt they had to beg for sex from their wives, who would rather be watching TV. The one couple who had four children and were expecting a fifth, were a little pudgy, a little bargain-shoppish in appearance and a little financially stressed. They listened to their siblings and their spouses with incomprehension; their sex life, interrupted not uncommonly by sick or needy kids, was frequent and satisfying. The fatigue of home-schooling and stretching a limited income had not encroached upon their lovemaking.

And maybe that is the clue. They thought of having sex not as "having sex" but as "making love." Not that the others didn't love each other, but sex for them had become routine and not the occasion of making an emphatic statement of love to each other. The pill had enabled them to have sex before marriage, and sex had become simply one more pleasurable act without much meaning. The couple who were also parents had retained the ability to recognize the act of having sex as a profound expression of love; one of the reasons that their sexual acts could express that meaning was their respect for the baby-making power of the sexual act. When couples who are willing to have a baby make love to one another, they are expressing a willingness to have their whole lives bound up together: "I love you so much; I am willing to be a parent with you." The act itself is laden with the meanings of affirmation and commitment. Contraceptive sex significantly undermines that meaning. By its very nature it expresses the intent not to become a parent with the other. While couples who use contraception may in fact love one another deeply, contracepted sex expresses a willingness only to engage in a momentary physical pleasure and thus expresses neither love nor commitment. The body language of contraception therefore works against the very love which sex is meant to express and cultivate.

Consider Natural Family Planning

And lest critics wail that women are not baby-making machines, mention must be made of truly green forms of child-spacing methods of natural family planning (NFP). Modern methods of NFP enable a woman to determine with great reliability the generally 7–10 days a month she is fertile and is not to be confused with the old "rhythm method," which relied on counting days on a calendar. Requiring no chemicals, totally without harmful physical or environmental effects (consider the carbon footprint of chemical contraceptives), and costing nothing to use, methods of NFP have proven as effective as any form of contraception. They also respect the baby-making power of sex by not treating fertility as some bodily defect that must be corrected. Most couples who use NFP have contracepted at one time and readily testify that their lovemaking when using NFP is markedly different in quality from their having contracepted sex.

So instead of supplementing one pill with another, women should go green in their sex lives. Not only will they protect the delicate ecology of their female fertility from libido-reducing chemicals, they may find themselves tickled pink with their sex lives.

> *"For the first time, mainstream culture and the Left may be forced to take a look at the side effects of oral contraceptives."*

The Birth Control Pill Has Destructive Environmental Consequences

Kathryn Lopez

Kathryn Lopez is the editor of National Review Online. *In the following viewpoint, she contends that evidence shows that the birth control pill may be causing some serious environmental damage. As estrogen from the pill enters the nation's water supply, fish have shown up with physical malformations and defects. Lopez wonders if these dire environmental consequences will finally force a reevaluation of the birth control pill and lead to its reclassification as a pollutant.*

As you read, consider the following questions:

1. In which body of water were male largemouth bass appearing with eggs in their sex organs, according to Lopez?

2. What does author Iain Murray predict will be the reaction of environmental groups to new evidence about the pill's pollution?

3. According to Murray, how has the United Kingdom classified the birth control pill?

You've already heard about the pregnant man. But what about the she-man fish? "Intersex" freshwater fish are all the rage. But unlike the pregnant man, these scaly androgynies didn't ask to take on the sexual characteristics of both genders: Humans are doing it to them. (Where's the freedom to choose?!) And the reason these fish are doubling up could make hash of orthodoxies dating back to the sexual revolution.

Estrogen pollution from contraceptive and abortion pills could be the culprit behind these piscine switcheroos. And thus the two holiest of holies for the Left may be on a collision course. It promises to be quite the show.

Starting a few years ago, in the Potomac River, male largemouth bass started popping up with eggs in their sex organs. The deformity usually makes reproduction impossible, ultimately hurting the fish population. Many scientists believe the problem could stem from hormones and other pollutants flushed into our nation's waterways from sewage treatment plants.

The Environmental Effect of the Pill

In his book *The Really Inconvenient Truths: Seven Environmental Catastrophes Liberals Don't Want You to Know About— Because They Helped Cause Them* (Regnery, 2008), Iain Murray writes: "Why don't we have more outcries about hormones, and campaigns to save the fish populations? Why aren't environmentalists lobbying on Capitol Hill to keep these chemicals from being dumped into our rivers?" He answers his own question: "Maybe because the source of these chemicals is not some corporate polluter, but something a little more dear to the Left: human birth-control pills, morning-after pills, and abortion pills."

The contraceptive pill has fundamentally changed American life, making sex more casual, morals looser, husbands and wives more distant. It's messed with women's fertility. In short, it has been a game-changer, in some fundamental and not-so-good ways. And because its introduction came 40 years ago, at a time when American culture was enamored with Woodstock, feminism and free love, prescient warnings and cautions—most notably from Pope Paul VI in his encyclical "Humanae Vitae" in the summer of 1968—went unheeded.

The Complicity of Environmental Groups

But we may soon have reason to regret our embrace of the little white pill. For the first time, mainstream culture and the Left may be forced to take a look at the side effects of oral contraceptives. Never mind the women, of course. Never mind the men and children affected in various emotional and other ways. The fish! Have mercy on the fish!

The turnaround won't come, however, without some whiplash. Ironically, the environmental groups have long been on the same page as the abortion-industry foot soldiers, embracing anything that assuages fears of overpopulation (no longer a worry, as Western countries, particularly in Europe, face plummeting birth rates). "The protection of the quality of our environment is impossible in the face of the present rate of population growth," and therefore, "Laws, policies, and attitudes that foster population growth or big families, or that restrict abortion and contraception . . . should be abandoned; [and] comprehensive and realistic birth control programs should be available to every member of our society." That's not from Planned Parenthood; it's a Sierra Club resolution from 1970.

This is from Planned Parenthood: "Prominent women in the global environmental movement ... believe there are strong links between the health of the environment, the ability of women to engage and lead their communities, and their ability to exercise their inherent reproductive rights. Women have a stake in a clean environment because they are often the main providers of food and water, and their reproductive health can be adversely affected by environmental degradation."

But, Murray writes, "By any standard typically used by environmentalists, the pill is a pollutant. It does the same thing, just worse, as other chemicals they call pollutants."

Denial of the Problem

So what does that mean for us and the fish? Nothing straightaway, Murray tells me. There's more than pollution at stake here for the Left, so, expect "outright denial at there being a problem, obfuscation of the science when strong arguments are presented, attempts to deflect attention onto much rarer and less harmful industrial estrogen, and ad hominem accusations, in this case an allegation of religious zealotry/being in the pay of the 'very well-funded pro-life industry' I imagine. The effort will be based on making it unacceptable to bring up the issue in polite conversation, such that anyone who does so will end up stigmatized (astonishing how often the Left resorts to shame, rather than thinking about guilt). Some radical Greens may actually be honest enough to admit there is a problem. They will be marginalized by the environmental-industrial-entertainment complex (to paraphrase Fox Mulder [fictional character from the TV series *The X-Files*])."

With the science out there, Murray argues solving the problem wouldn't be out of the realm of possibility if we could all be adult about it. "The EPA [Environmental Protection Agency] and FDA [US Food and Drug Administration] (ought) to have the courage to do what their counterparts in the U.K. [United Kingdom] had the courage to do and label the pill as the pollutant it is."

Choice needs to be based on information; it should always be the result of thoughtful deliberation. When you interfere with a natural process, there are consequences, not all of them good—and you should be mindful of them. It's not just fish that end up getting hurt.

> *"Millions of metric tons of chemical substances are imported to or produced in the United States on a daily basis—in light of this, our use of contraceptives seems to be a drop in the bucket."*

The Birth Control Pill's Environmental Impact Is Relatively Small

Anna C. Christensen

Anna C. Christensen is a blogger and regular contributor to the Planned Parenthood Advocates of Arizona blog. In the following viewpoint, she observes that birth control pills have been blamed unfairly for introducing endocrine-disrupting chemicals (EDCs) into the environment. Christensen contends that EDCs can be found in a wide range of other products, including pesticides, detergents, herbicides, and cosmetics. One strategy to curb the presence of EDCs in our environment is developing microbes capable of breaking them down in soil or the water supply. To blame the birth control pill for EDCs instead of industrial pollution and other processes goes against the available evidence.

As you read, consider the following questions:

1. According to Christensen, how can EDCs disrupt an organism's endocrine system?

2. How much estrogen does the author say pregnant women can excrete a day?

3. How much pesticide is used every year, according to estimates?

The birth control pill has given millions of people the ability to decide whether and when to have children, and its arrival on the scene in 1960 coincided with increasing concern about population growth—so not only was it seen as a force of liberation for women, it was also seen as a tool to stem the tide of the world's expanding population. Many proponents of zero population growth thought they could end poverty and hunger through the stabilization of the population—as well as conserve the earth's finite resources. Lately, however, the birth control pill and other hormonal contraceptives have received negative attention for their apparent ability to introduce endocrine disruptors into the environment.

What Are EDCs?

Endocrine-disrupting chemicals (EDCs) get their name from their ability to interfere with an organism's endocrine system, which regulates hormones, or a body's "chemical messengers." This can wreak hormonal havoc on wildlife, affecting their development, fertility, and immunity. Therefore, EDCs have the potential to decrease or eliminate entire populations of creatures that happened to live in the wrong place at the wrong time.

Hormones work by binding to a complementary receptor. Depending on the hormone and the cell type, a reaction is triggered—perhaps a cell is prompted to synthesize an enzyme, or cell division is stimulated. Sex hormones, such as androgen and estrogen, are responsible for inducing the development of secondary sex characteristics, among other things. There are many mechanisms by which EDCs can disrupt an organism's endocrine system: They can "trick" a body into recognizing it as a hormone; they can interfere with the function, production, or use of an organism's natural hormones; or they can interfere with an organism's hormone receptors.

EDCs started to receive serious attention in the literature in the 1990s. Many chemicals can act as EDCs, including natural estrogens from humans or other animals, as well as synthetic estrogens, including ethinylestradiol, and chemicals with "estrogenic activities," such as nonylphenol and other alkylphenols, phthalates and other plasticizers, and polychlorinated biphenyls. Other chemicals with the capacity to disrupt endocrine systems of wildlife include organochlorine pesticides and certain pharmaceutical compounds.

EDCs: The Case Against Them

Before we examine hormonal birth control and its ecological impact, let's look at the charges that have been brought against EDCs. You might have already heard about the pesticide atrazine and its feminizing effects on male frogs. Natural and synthetic estrogens seem to have similar effects on male fish after entering rivers as part of sewage effluent. Both natural and synthetic estrogens can bind to estrogen receptors of aquatic animals and interfere with their own bodies' biological processes. The synthetic 17α-ethinylestradiol (a component of oral contraceptives), as well as nonylphenol (a chemical with wide applications that is used in spermicides such as nonoxynol-9), can induce vitellogenesis—the production of a female yolk protein—in male fish, which is the most reported effect of estrogenic chemicals in the waterways. The UK Environment Agency conducted two large-scale studies in which thousands of fish from across the country were examined, and a correlation was found between even low levels of estrogen in the water and vitellogenesis in male fish, which itself was linked to reduced fertility in these populations.

EDCs need not mimic estrogen; for example, metabolites of pesticides such as vinclozolin and DDT have been found to have anti-androgenic effects on organisms. By binding to an organism's androgen receptors, these chemicals can block the actions of testosterone. Tributyltin, a component of a paint used on the hulls of ships, is a frequently cited EDC; it can masculinize female mollusks and has almost driven some populations to extinction—and it has been banned in many parts of the world.

The Chemicals in Birth Control

As you can see, the synthetic hormones in our birth control aren't the only sources for EDCs—chemicals from a wide variety of other compounds can have endocrine-disrupting effects on wildlife. But let's look specifically at the synthetic estrogens that arise from our contraceptive toolkit. In experiments, estrogens have been shown to be "the most biologically potent" of the EDCs. While the majority of 17β-estradiol and 17α-ethinylestradiol break down very quickly, the trace amounts that don't degrade tend to persist in the environment. One group of researchers referred to 17α-ethinylestradiol, a synthetic estrogen used in combined contraceptives such as the pill, the patch, and the ring, as "particularly recalcitrant"—it can accumulate in the soil, wastewater, water sediments, and groundwater.

Let's look at nonylphenol as well—while its use as a spermicide is dwarfed by its wider use in detergents, emulsifiers, wetting agents, herbicides, and cosmetics, we can still consider the impact it might have as a part of our birth control arsenal. Nonoxynol is used in spermicide and as a lubricant in condoms; it breaks down into nonylphenol, which has also been found to be estrogenic and can end up in waterways.

What about estrogen sources that are first disposed of in landfills? The ring (e.g., NuvaRing) is composed of a polymer called polyethylene vinyl acetate and its active ingredients are etonogestrel and ethinylestradiol. After three weeks of use, an estimated 85 percent of ethinylestradiol remains present in the ring—almost 2.4 mg (down from the original 2.7 mg).

What does this mean for the ecosystem? A Dutch team (in a study specific to the landfill systems, contraceptive usage, and rainfall patterns of the Netherlands) determined that the ethinylestradiol used in NuvaRing has a negligible effect on the environment when disposed of in landfills. It leaches from the ring very slowly, and the sandy soil underneath a landfill can absorb ethinylestradiol, further reducing chances of groundwater contamination. Ethinylestradiol can stay in sandy soil for many years before eventually reaching groundwater; by this time the remainder could have been degraded by microbial or other processes.

Other Sources for EDCs

We must look at the deleterious effects of contraceptive-derived EDCs in the greater context. Millions of metric tons of chemical substances are imported to or produced in the United States on a *daily* basis—in light of this, our use of contraceptives seems to be a drop in the bucket. Other chemicals with estrogenic activity include alkylphenols and bisphenol A (BPA), which have estrogenic potencies far lower than those of natural and synthetic estrogens, yet their prevalence in the environment is at a much higher concentration.

Furthermore, natural estrogen gets into the environment at even greater rates than do synthetic estrogens from contraceptives. Women excrete estrogen every day—more or less depending on their cycle. Pregnant women can excrete up to 30 mg of estrogen a day, and this accumulates in the environment as well.

How Green Are Condoms?

Because condoms are the only effective method besides abstinence for preventing sexually transmitted infections, giving them up is absolutely not an option for anyone at risk of these problems. Environmental organizations, including EPA [Environmental Protection Agency], have worried about improper condom disposal. The Ocean Conservancy, a nonprofit group based in Washington, DC, estimates that 30,252 condoms are picked up on beaches each year, and the devices are among the many pollutants making up the growing amount of sea trash disrupting coral reefs and ocean ecosystems.

Laura Eldridge,
"Adding Environmental Footprints to Birth Control Choices,"
On the Issues, *Spring 2011.*

Female humans aren't the only organisms loosing their estrogen-laden urine into the environment. Agricultural sources of EDCs—fertilizers, pesticides, herbicides, sewage, and other minerals—have the greatest potential for ecological damage. The increasing industrialization and centralization of agriculture is responsible for large amounts of livestock waste entering the water in rural areas. Steroids, such as growth "enhancers" in cattle, are used regularly in agriculture. Pregnant mammals, such as those used for livestock, excrete estrogens, which themselves can affect aquatic and terrestrial species. Agricultural effluent is often disposed of by being spread over fields—untreated! There is so much of it that it cannot be adequately processed by the soils and can either find its way into groundwater or into waterways as runoff.

The majority of EDCs are pesticides—it is estimated that 5 billion tons of pesticides are used every year, and many pesticides have been found to have estrogenic activity. If they don't bind to the soil they can find themselves in the waterways. According to the USGS [US Geological Survey], pesticides such as atrazine are found in 57 percent of streams in the United States.

Strategies for Treating or Reducing EDCs

EDCs are not completely removed during the sewage treatment process—but they could be. A search through the literature reveals piles of studies by scientists investigating microbes capable of breaking down EDCs into their inert constituents—if these microbes were used in wastewater treatment, we would be releasing cleaner waste water into the environment. Residues of EDCs in the waterways depend on a municipality's wastewater treatment systems; unless you know about your local water treatment system's efficacy, you can't know how much harm you are doing with the pharmaceutical and personal care products you are washing down the drain.

While microbes in sewage systems are much more effective than soil microbes in degrading free estrogens, wild microbes in the soil can also break down some of these chemicals before they reach the groundwater, adding another line of defense against contamination. Despite the "recalcitrance" of 17α-ethinylestradiol, some microbes exhibit the ability to degrade it quickly; for example, in one study *Rhodococcus zopfii* (strain Y50158) was able to degrade 17α-ethinylestradiol completely within 24 hours. An enzyme from horseradish also did quite well with natural and synthetic estrogens, degrading most or all of them within an hour, under the right conditions. We already have strategies to effect the breakdown of EDCs—we just have to put these tools to use.

The difficulties involved in testing the effects of chemicals are complicated by the additive or synergistic effects that chemicals might have in combination—normally, when chemicals are tested they are done so in isolation from one another.

> *"All of this talk about a male pill has reopened the debate about why it's not yet available."*

A Male Birth Control Pill Would Give Men More Control over Reproductive Choices

Michael Parsons

Michael Parsons is the pseudonym of a writer who contributes to Role/Reboot. In the following viewpoint, the author looks forward to the development of a male birth control pill because it would give him more control over reproductive choices. The author's life, he explains, was impacted by an unplanned pregnancy. A male birth control pill would have given him the opportunity to take more responsibility for family planning decisions. He argues that the time is right for men to have male contraception.

As you read, consider the following questions:

1. How long have rumors of a male birth control pill been circulating, according to the author?

2. According to the author, how does the nature camp explain the lack of a male birth control pill?

3. How did the author remedy his personal situation?

I'm a member of a small, but increasing minority: the stay-at-home father. Like stay-at-home mothers always have, I've put aside my professional ambitions and earning power to be the primary caregiver for our children. I'm not saying that I would change that. I really love my kids and wouldn't trade places with anyone in the world, but the sacrifices are significant. As a man whose life course was altered by an unexpected pregnancy, Tracy Clark-Flory's recent *Salon* article "What will 'the male pill' change?" struck a chord.

The Dirt on the Male Birth Control Pill

Let's start with the reality: There is still no male pill or any equivalent male contraceptive today, nor is there likely to be one in the near future. Over the past 20 years, there have been countless reports of imminent breakthroughs in male artificial contraception, ranging from pills to implants to shots, all designed to prevent sperm from reaching an egg with minimal side effects to the sperm producer. And yet, despite all this talk, not a single product of this type has been brought to market. The "male pill" article ends on a sober note, quoting the inventor of the female oral contraceptive saying: "I do not see the faintest chance of [a male pill] being approved in the next couple of decades."

All of this talk about a male pill has reopened the debate about why it's not yet available. Like many debates involving gender politics, the discussion often breaks down into nature vs. nurture arguments. The nature camp argues that it is not surprising that male contraception has languished because it is more difficult to safely incapacitate the male reproductive system. The nurture side believes that the real impediment is *attitudes* about male contraception, both in term[s of] how

The Male Birth Control Pill and Cultural Attitudes

No matter how "emasculating" people think it might be, the male pill will be a real alternative to pulling out and vasectomies and would give monogamous couples much more reliable birth control. Since the male pill would signal a man as virile and sexually active, it would sell like crazy. And for those with a fragile male self-image, just consider the increased male responsibility, normalization of birth control and reduced accidental pregnancies as fringe benefits.

Kyle Munkittrick,
"Why I Want a Male Birth Control Pill,"
Discover Magazine, *March 28, 2011.*

men and women negotiate responsibility for birth control and the attitudes of pharmaceutical companies about men's propensity to take responsibility for this decision. Wherever you choose to place the blame, the lack of a male pill is a huge disappointment, because there's an increasing number of men (and women)—including myself—who would love to have greater control over the reproductive future of our families. I see my own experience as indicative of why this is the case.

My Story

Eight years ago, we had three boys: 8, 6, and 5 (all planned, more or less). My wife was working and I was at home. She was on the pill. After 8 years of not working outside the home, I was planning to return to my career in the fall, when all of the boys would be in school. However, just a month before school started, my wife came home and said she was pregnant. For some unknown reason, the pill had failed. I was in a daze for weeks, scrapping all my plans to finally go back to work, and feeling both stupid and helpless. I'm a well-educated adult, but at the time I felt like a 17-year-old girl who'd gotten knocked up in the backseat of a car.

Despite my shock, life went on. My wife gave birth the following spring and went back to work after a few months. I stayed home, where I remain today. Now, I don't want to seem like I'm complaining. I'm well aware I could have used a condom to be extra careful. But it would have been wonderful if a male pill had been available to me as a simple and effective means of contraception. As it was, after the birth my wife tried to return to the pill, but its increasing side effects forced her to stop taking it. After that we agreed that I would be primarily responsible for birth control, and I was—being very, very careful and using condoms.

Our fourth son really solidified our "role reversal" in my household. Feminists will be forgiven for chuckling at our situation: simply put, to my wife, sex was now mostly about recreation while for me it involved mostly (preventing) procreation. The unplanned pregnancy did not set her career plans back much, but it had devastating consequences for mine. After three years of diligence and condoms, I had a vasectomy, which finally leveled the playing field (at least in the bedroom).

I'm very happy and proud to be a father of four. I'm very lucky that we can afford our lifestyle on my wife's salary. But having a safe, reliable male contraceptive would have given me a measure of greater control over my life. Unfortunately for all of us, it still seems to be a wish and a hope.

The question I want to ask is: How will things change if we *don't* get a male pill? After all, the world is changing. Gender roles are no longer functioning as they used to. Men and women no longer approach parenthood and careers with the same expectations that ruled society in previous generations. The number of stay-at-home dads and breadwinner moms is increasing. I think you'll agree: It's about time for men to have more control over their reproductive futures, as well.

> *"That it [the male birth control pill]*
> *won't compare to the upheaval brought*
> *by the Pill isn't to say that it won't have*
> *a significant cultural impact."*

A Male Birth Control Pill Could Lead to Less Responsible Sexual Behavior

Tracy Clark-Flory

Tracy Clark-Flory is a staff writer at Salon. *In the following viewpoint, she explores the impact that a male birth control pill might have for men. After interviewing a range of experts on the topic, she reports that most do not believe it will have the profound effect that the female birth control pill had for women in the 1960s and 1970s. In fact, she reports, a few experts predict that it will allow men to aspire to have sex with different partners, since they do not have to worry about unplanned pregnancies. Another possible outcome, Clark-Flory maintains, is that infidelity would become even more common.*

As you read, consider the following questions:

1. According to the author, what percentage of men say they would be interested in taking a male birth control pill?

2. What does historian Andrew Russell say about the effect of the male birth control pill?

3. When does Carl Djerassi predict that a male birth control pill will be developed?

The birth control pill changed everything for women, allowing greater freedom to pursue higher education, careers and, yes, sex. Now just imagine what kind of social change a contraceptive for men would bring.

That's one question that has largely been ignored amid a recent upswell in buzz about promising scientific advances in the search for "the male pill"—just as it is every time this perennial topic is raised. Once again, the conversation centers on why we don't have it already (Big Pharma doesn't see it as profitable), how soon this innovation will happen (the joke in the medical community: It's been five years away for the past 30 years) and whether or not men will actually go for it (50 percent say they're interested). If we're going to try to make social forecasts based on a hypothetical future innovation, we might as well consider the more compelling issue of what it could mean for relationships and sex.

So, I went to a range of experts—from anthropologists to sociologists to sexologists (and even some not ending in "-ogist")—and asked them to, well, predict the future.

What the Experts Say

Sorry, fellas, but they do not prophesize a sexual revolution comparable to the one brought about by the Pill. No big surprise there, right? As historian Andrew Russell told me, "The liberating effect of the Pill in the 1960s was magnified in

Birth Control Pills and the Rainbow Trout

[Biologist John] Woodling, University of Colorado physiology professor David Norris, and their EPA [Environmental Protection Agency]-study team were among the first scientists in the country to learn that a slurry of hormones, antibiotics, caffeine and steroids is coursing down the nation's waterways, threatening fish and contaminating drinking water.

Since their findings, stories have been emerging everywhere. Scientists in western Washington found that synthetic estrogen—a common ingredient in oral contraceptives—drastically reduces the fertility of male rainbow trout.

Wayne Laugesen,
"Contracepting the Environment,"
National Catholic Register, July 10, 2007.

many ways by the distance that it created between that decade and the repressive norms of the 1950s and earlier decades," he says. "I don't think the 2010s need emboldened men as much as the 1960s needed liberated women." Elaine Lissner, director of the Male Contraception Information Project, agrees: "It'll be more subtle, because when the Pill was introduced, you were starting closer to zero."

That it won't compare to the upheaval brought by the Pill isn't to say that it won't have a significant cultural impact. Carol Queen, a Good Vibrations staff sexologist, told me that it might allow men to "aspire" to have more sex, perhaps with more partners. She says this "may free up women to further explore sexual possibilities" as well as "further challenge monogamy and hasten the open discussion of positive alternatives to monogamy." Most experts expect it would decrease the rate of unplanned pregnancies, but Queen suggests that comes with the risk that "contraception will feel more immediate and necessary than safer sex prophylaxis." The result could be "that pill-popping males may be even less inclined to use condoms," she says, "maybe especially when they're out on the town, not at home with partners where they'll have to wonder what room to put the bassinet in if sperm should meet egg."

The Role of Infidelity

That raises the dreaded issue of infidelity: A male birth control pill could certainly come as a relief to cheaters who would rather not have their lives complicated by a so-called "love child." A man who expects to stray but doesn't trust himself to reliably use a condom could rely on a long-term form of birth control, one that doesn't have to be taken as a pill every day. While on the subject of lies and deception, we might as well consider that it would be of great comfort to men who worry about partners intentionally missing pills in order to get pregnant without their consent, as well as those troubled by that classic male problem of paternity uncertainty. In an AskMen .com message board conversation about the potential for "the male pill," one user writes, "i want to be there the first time a girl says to her bf 'im pregnant, we need to get married' and he goes 'well it cant be mine, so have fun marrying the other guy.'"

On a cheerier note, Lissner says, "One group we see really wanting this is men whose wives or partners are having trouble with female methods and they want to be able to do their part." She argues that it will be ideal for "modern men who want to be able to do more for their partners"—and in doing more for them, it could certainly lead to happier relationships.

Taking Responsibility

Queen is most interested to see whether a male contraceptive will mean that men will "begin to identify more as responsible for any potential pregnancy," she says. "If women were to have men around who would gladly step up to the plate on this issue, it would, perhaps, shift a ground-level dynamic in male-female relationships having to do with power and trust." That could have a profound impact on the way that we approach reproductive rights in this country. Consider, for example, the recent argument over whether insurance companies should be required to cover birth control as preventative care: A male contraceptive would evade the opposition's argument that certain forms of birth control are actually abortion. "As far as the abortion issue, this is about as far away from an egg as you can get," says Lissner. "Only if you believe that every sperm is sacred and no seed should be spilled can you be against a method like this"—or if like the Catholic Church you oppose "artificial" contraception.

A Matter of Trust

Typically, women have had extra motivation as the caregiver to prevent unplanned pregnancies, but Linda Gordon, a history professor at New York University, points out that men are increasingly sharing parental responsibility. She says, "I think the main reason people want to have fewer children now is economic, so I think that's going to give men more incentive." Still, it's the woman whose body is transformed by pregnancy and, indeed, Gordon points to a survey by one of her students showing that women—or at least female college students— trust men less than men trust women to reliably take oral contraceptives. In fact, "a lot of men don't trust themselves," Gordon, author of *Woman's Body, Woman's Right: A Social History of Birth Control in America*, says. "They will say, quite frankly, that they think they're not as disciplined as women are with things having to do with sexual reproduction."

It may be some time yet before we find out for sure. Despite the recent flurry of optimistic press coverage, Carl Djerassi, a chemist who helped develop the very first oral contraceptive, says there are impassable practical, economic and legal obstacles still in the way. In an e-mail, he told me, "I do not see the faintest chance of one being approved in the next couple of decades."

> "A male birth control pill would be as odd and contrary to the broader biological and social conditions as females raping males or the cab driver going directly to your destination using the shortest possible route."

A Male Birth Control Pill Violates Biological and Social Imperatives

Greg Laden

Greg Laden is a blogger, writer, and scholar. In the following viewpoint, he maintains that there has been little push for the male birth control pill because it is women who are in control of reproduction in mammalian species, including humans. Giving men some of that control, Laden argues, goes against biological and social drives that are inherent in our species. Laden finds that a male birth control pill would be a good idea, but he doubts it will happen soon because of cultural attitudes toward reproductive control.

As you read, consider the following questions:

1. How does Laden describe the role of males in the reproductive process of most mammals?

2. In Laden's cab analogy, who is the driver and who is the passenger?

3. How does the author's story about the printer-and-scanner party relate to the male birth control pill?

Why is there no birth control pill for men?

The answer I'd like to propose can be summed up in two closely linked words pilfered from the question itself:

Men. Control.

Myriad aspects of life can be understood by recognizing a single critical fact, and the layered, sometimes complex, deeply biological effects of that fact. Males, by definition, *can't have babies.*

The Male Role in Reproduction

All mammalian males contribute to the reproductive endeavor, but often this contribution consists of a single cell, one per offspring. True, that cell contains a haploid copy of the male's DNA, the quality of which is critically important to the female. In contrast, nutrients for the fetus (through blood), nutrients for the infant (through lactation), protection from the elements, protection from predators, protection from infanticidal males, and transmission of biologically critical knowledge is provided by the female alone in the majority of mammal species. In these species the reproductive role of males is pre-copulation, and of course the deed itself. Precopulatory activity consists of direct competition with other males for sexual access to one or more females, or showy demonstration before the observing females of the qualities likely to be associated with that single cell, the sperm cell, that contains the male's genes.

Otherwise, the best a male can do to help the little ones grow and mature is to get out of Dodge and stay out of the way. Males that hang around after sex are a bother. They eat the food and they attract predators. Nobody wants them.

Parental Behavior in Mammals

Evolutionary psychologists often take the circumstance of nearly zero male investment as the starting point for theorizing about human sexual strategies and social organization. "Males are selected to inseminate as many females as possible," is a stock phrase.

Well, it is a starting point, but only in the way that a nice red rock and some mineral oil is the starting point for an expensive tube of lipstick. The male as gladiator and sperm donor (and little else) might be the most common trope among mammals, but it is also true that a lot of mammalian species exhibit male parental care to varying degrees, and humans are this sort of mammal. More paternal care, longer periods of investment, and the greater reproductive value of each individual offspring means there will be more serious risk to males making bad investment choices. The females are at risk of reproductive failure as well (in fact, ultimately, females are usually at greater risk than males), but they have access to the most direct means of controlling reproduction. We would therefore expect human males to be the most neurotic . . . in an evolutionary sense . . . about making babies.

Female mammals are in direct control of reproduction, but male mammals are never in direct control. Males are therefore forced to adhere to either Plan A . . . get out of Dodge . . . or Plan B. Control the females.

Control Issues in Reproduction

When I say that female mammals are in control, I mean this in reference to every part of the process. In most mammal species, females choose with whom to have sex to a much greater degree than any male aardvark or high school student would like to admit. Females choose whether or not the egg will be inseminated. Females choose to allow the egg to be implanted. Females choose whether or not a fetus will grow or be aborted. Females choose how much to nurse their offspring. Here, I take liberties with the word "choose." We could be talking about a physiological response to maternal condition that biases the likelihood of fertilization by an X- vs. Y-toting sperm (in elk), or a conversation among friends that supports a decision to go out on a second date with a particular suitor (in humans).

For every way in which females are in control, Plan B males (including humans) should be selected to exert indirect control in some corresponding way. In "monogamous" mammal species, this may be in the form of total exclusion of all other reproductive males from a territory, and constant attendance to the female. In social mammals, a male's indirect control of the reproductive process may be much more varied to meet the circumstances.

Human males can rape. They can coerce. They can arrange for the marriage between their kin and the kin of an ally. Male judges can order the sterilization of individual females or a whole class of females, and male generals and privates can carry out a little genocide here, a little rape and murder there. Males can pass laws that limit a woman's access to day-to-day birth control methods, to abortion, and to possession of property (resources). These are the ways that males can determine, at several different levels, the outcome of female reproductive activities.

A Cab Analogy for Reproductive Control

It's like taking a cab in San Francisco. The driver is the metaphorical female, the hapless passenger from Boston is the metaphorical male. The cab driver has control of the actual driving . . . the gas, the brakes, the steering wheel, the gear

"I hear there's a new birth control pill for men," cartoon by Mike Flanagan, www .CartoonStock.com. Copyright © Mike Flanagan. Reproduction rights obtainable from www.CartoonStock.com.

shift. The passenger can get what he wants only using indirect means. You can scream at the cab driver or you can pay the cab driver off, but you can't drive the cab.

There are other ways that males can influence reproduction. In some species, males can use the strategy of being nice. Baboons within a given "troop" seem to fluctuate between being tough and being nice, depending on age and rank of the male. The situation is roughly similar in humans, but less complex. Social rules vary wildly across human societies, but individual males simply have to learn as they grow up what the social rules are and either follow them or be very, very good at breaking them. Influential institutions and individuals, historical circumstance, and economics may cause changes in human societies over fairly short periods of time. The degree of male coercion vs. male niceness can shift for a lot of reasons. But a given male usually just has to watch the big boys and do what they do.

The female birth control pill is an excellent way of controlling reproduction, but it has some costs, which are all borne by the female. It allows females to be sexually receptive with less risk for making bad decisions, which is beneficial to the strategy of both the male and female. But it interferes with only the female's physiology and it has health risks only for the female. The male remains fecund. The male can still philander, but he cannot be a cuckold.

Going Against Nature

A male birth control pill would be as odd and contrary to the broader biological and social conditions as females raping males or the cab driver going directly to your destination using the shortest possible route. Virtually unthinkable.

But there is hope. I would say, in the absence of any information about the physiological or health-related side effects, that a male birth control pill would be a good idea. But it is a good idea in the same way that not owning women as though they were cattle is a good idea. This idea that women should be socially, politically, and economically equivalent to men is a very, very new concept, and is only now being put into place, and in fact is very rare on this planet today.

I'm reminded of two conversations, one I had with a computer engineer 20 years ago, and one I saw between John Stossel and Bella Abzug on a documentary from the late 1980s. . . .

A Perpetual Motion Machine

In the first conversation, the computer engineer and his wife (an archaeologist) had a party to celebrate their recent purchase and successful installation of a printer and a scanner.

Those were the old days, before printers and scanners were routinely provided free with your computer. The expensive devices (with the computer) had their own table in their own room, off the dining room. In the dining room were munchies and drinks, and guests would get their victuals and wander in groups of two or three into this special room to see a demonstration conducted by the proud parents.

After I saw the demonstration, a thought occurred to me, which I (as usual) blurted out: "Hey, some day there will be a machine that scans and prints, and it can be a fax machine too, and it will be cheap enough that we'll all have one."

Ooops. The host was deeply offended. He went on at length about all of the reasons this could never happen. There were fundamental, unbreakable laws of physics and engineering that would make such a machine impossible. I may as well have suggested a perpetual motion machine to Lord Kelvin himself.

Today, when I hear about the impossibility of designing a male birth control pill, I recall this conversation.

Stossel vs. Abzug

The second conversation, between the smart-ass *20/20* reporter John Stossel and feminist New York congresswoman Bella Abzug, went like this:

Stossel (smirking): "So, you are saying if women want to be firefighters but need physical assistance in their jobs, they should actually be given physical assistance of some kind?"

Abzug (dead serious): "Right. If you need to invent an electric axe, invent an electric axe!"

Periodical and Internet Sources Bibliography

The following articles have been selected to supplement the diverse views presented in this chapter.

Laura Eldridge	"Adding Environmental Footprints to Birth Control Choices," *On the Issues*, Spring 2011.
Laura Eldridge	"The Dark Side of Birth Control: The Pill Still Has Many Adverse Affects Glossed Over by Big Pharma," AlterNet, March 17, 2010. www.alternet.org.
Shelley Gao	"The GAO Report: Celebration of Women," *Stanford Daily*, May 10, 2010.
Amanda Gardner	"The Pill Turns 50," *US News & World Report*, May 7, 2010.
Kate Harding	"Are Men Too Incompetent to Use the Male Pill?," *Salon*, January 12, 2010. www.salon.com.
Kyle Munkittrick	"Why I Want a Male Birth Control Pill," *Discover Magazine*, March 28, 2011.
Iain Murray	"The Pill as Pollutant," *National Review Online*, April 22, 2008. www.nationalreview.com.
Christiane Northrup	"The Pill Turns 50: Taking Stock," *Huffington Post*, April 22, 2010. www.huffingtonpost.com.
Sarah Paeth	"Contraceptives May Soon Become a Two-Person Responsibility," *Daily Barometer*, January 11, 2011.
Rita Rubin	"The Pill: 50 Years of Birth Control Changed Women's Lives," *USA Today*, May 8, 2010.
Rex Sexton	"Estrogen Pollution: A Potential Human-Health Disaster," United Church of God, August 14, 2008. www.ucg.org.

How Should Access to Birth Control Be Managed?

Chapter Preface

A conscience clause is an exemption for doctors, pharmacists, or health care professionals that allows them to refuse to provide services to certain patients for religious or moral reasons. In such cases, they argue that dispensing drugs or providing medical services goes against their conscience or religious beliefs. One example of conscience clause is a physician who refuses to perform an abortion because it goes against his or her moral views. Another example is a pharmacist who will not provide emergency contraception because he or she believes that it causes an abortion. There has been a continuing controversy over whether and under what circumstances the government should allow pharmacists to interfere in the reproductive choices of individuals and refuse to provide legal drugs for women.

The first conscience clause was passed by the US Congress in 1973 to address the practice of abortion, which had just become legal weeks earlier. Senator Frank Church proposed legislation to prevent the federal government from requiring health care providers or institutions to perform or assist in abortion procedures if they objected for moral or religious reasons. Known as the Church amendment, it also ensured that institutions, including Catholic hospitals, could refuse to perform abortions or sterilization procedures without losing federal funds.

Building on the Church amendment, many states adopted conscience clauses of their own—and took it one step further. A number of these state conscience clauses allow health care providers and pharmacists the right to refuse to prescribe or dispense emergency contraception and even birth control pills. Others permit physicians to refuse to provide emergency health care services or to not tell their employers or patients that they will refuse to perform certain procedures or prescribe or dispense specific medications. In 2004 Congress passed the Hyde/Weldon Conscience Protection Amendment, which ensures that federal, state, or local governments cannot force any individual, institution, or payer to perform, provide, or pay for an abortion—nor can they be required to refer patients to another institution that would.

With the Weldon amendment, the ability to obstruct a patient's access to services was now a matter of conscience. Physicians and pharmacists not only began to deny service, they refused to provide referrals to other doctors or give information on where to find other pharmacies that would fill legal prescriptions. In some cases, doctors and pharmacies lectured patients seeking services on moral and religious issues. In 2004 Mississippi passed a clause that allows almost anyone connected with the health care industry to refuse to participate or assist in any kind of health care service without liability.

A 2008 George W. Bush administration regulation, known as the Provider Refusal Rule, went further in strengthening the ability of providers and institutions to refuse to offer services, even emergency medical procedures, that might result in abortion. It also directed that institutions that did not permit the conscience clause be denied federal funds. However, it inspired widespread condemnation when it included language that could be interpreted to redefine "abortion" as any action that prevents the implantation of a fertilized egg—which effectively would then include birth control pills, emergency contraception, and the intrauterine device (IUD). By effectively broadening the definition of abortion to include contraception, the Bush administration was making it much more difficult for women to have access to birth control.

Many health care organizations and associations opposed this change, and it was eventually revised. However, the Provider Refusal Rule had far-reaching impact. Some pharmacists refused to dispense prescriptions for HIV/AIDS medications;

pregnant women were refused drugs they needed for health reasons because they were pregnant; and other patients were refused insulin needles. All of these refusals were allegedly based on reasons of religion and conscience.

In 2007 the state of Washington passed new regulations to require pharmacists to ensure that patients get their prescriptions filled onsite in a timely manner, thereby eliminating the conscience clause for pharmacists. Several other states are considering passing similar legislation. In February 2011 the Barack Obama administration repealed the Provider Refusal Rule.

A pharmacist's right to refuse to dispense birth control is one of the topics explored in the following chapter, which examines how access to birth control should be managed. Other viewpoints in the chapter discuss recent proposals to provide universal birth control coverage and the question of religious exemptions for universal birth control coverage.

> "Requiring coverage of FDA-approved
> contraceptives like birth control pills,
> implants and IUDs and other neces-
> sary preventive services would seem like
> a no-brainer."

There Should Be Universal Birth Control Coverage

Laura W. Murphy

Laura W. Murphy is the director of the American Civil Liberties Union (ACLU) Washington Legislative Office. In the following viewpoint, she praises guidelines issued by the Department of Health and Human Services (HHS) in 2011 to require that contraception be covered by health insurance. Murphy notes that religious-based exemptions to the new policy, except for churches, synagogues, and other sectarian institutions, is antithetical to American values because it would impose religious values on health policy and deny women essential medical services. She applauds HHS for acknowledging the reality that women need and use contraception in contemporary American society.

As you read, consider the following questions:

1. What are some religious groups demanding in regard to the new policy, according to Murphy?

2. Why does the author feel that religiously affiliated institutions should not be able to refuse to cover birth control?

3. How many people do Catholic hospitals alone employ in the United States, according to the author?

Far too often, government policies tend to be at odds with reality when it comes to women's reproductive health by ignoring the services that women need most. Which is why guidelines recently issued by the Department of Health and Human Services [HHS] requiring insurance coverage for contraception and other preventive services were so welcome. After all, virtually every woman of childbearing age practices some sort of contraception at some point.

Requiring coverage of FDA [Food and Drug Administration]-approved contraceptives like birth control pills, implants and IUDs [intrauterine devices] and other necessary preventive services would seem like a no-brainer. Unfortunately, when it comes to health care in America today, nothing is ever that simple.

Opposition to Universal Birth Control Coverage

Following the HHS announcement, some groups have objected to the contraception requirement on religious grounds. They want a wide range of employers to get a special exception so they can deny their employees birth control coverage. The HHS guidelines already propose to exempt churches, synagogues and other exclusively sectarian institutions. But critics of the policy say that's not enough.

Public Attitudes Toward Birth Control

Approximately 8 in 10 (82%) Americans favor expanding access to birth control for women who cannot afford it, compared to only 16% who oppose it. Support is strong across all demographic religious and political groups, including the Tea Party.

Committed to Availability, Conflicted About Morality, *Washington, DC: Public Religion Research Institute, 2011, p. 18.*

These groups want special exceptions to allow any religiously affiliated institution, including hospitals that employ people of all faiths, to deny its employees insurance for birth control. If the critics had their way, the HHS guidelines would be meaningless for hundreds of thousands of women, who would lose the ability to determine which health services are best for them and their families and instead could be beholden to the religious beliefs of their employers.

Consider that Catholic hospitals alone employ over half a million people. The effects of broadening the exception would be sweeping.

Imposing Religious Beliefs

While everyone is free to make personal decisions regarding whether and when to use birth control, it is wrong for employers to force this decision on their employees by denying them access to essential health services.

This isn't the first time that religious groups have tried to impose their views on health policy. The U.S. Conference of Catholic Bishops tried to have contraception excluded from the guidelines altogether, denying these benefits to all women.

Currently, the bishops are pushing an even more extreme measure that could allow employers to refuse to provide coverage for any service they oppose, leaving health care coverage for thousands of people of all belief systems to the influence of one particular faith.

American Values

This is completely contrary to our values of both personal and religious freedom.

Women need, demand and utilize contraceptive services. This is the reality of women's health, and has been acknowledged and affirmed by the medical community and now by HHS. Those who oppose family planning cannot be permitted to allow their ideology to dictate others' health care. To do otherwise would mark a dismaying retreat from rationality in women's health policy.

> "The cultural Left assails 'culture warriors' while making it illegal for many cultural conservatives to live according to their conscience."

There Should Not Be Universal Birth Control Coverage

Timothy P. Carney

Timothy P. Carney is an author and the senior political columnist for the Washington Examiner. *In the following viewpoint, he regards the 2011 order to require insurance plans to cover contraception as an attack on morality and conscience and a giveaway to the pharmaceutical industry. Carney asserts that by mandating insurance coverage, the Barack Obama administration is rewarding a powerful lobby that has generously supported him. He also argues that the new policy offends Americans who do not use or support the use of contraception, especially emergency contraception.*

As you read, consider the following questions:

1. According to the author, how much money has the pharmaceutical industry spent on lobbying since 1998?

2. How much did Kathleen Sebelius receive from a biotech industry group for her support of embryo research, according to Carney?

3. Does the author say ella is more like RU-486 or Plan B?

President [Barack] Obama this week [July 24–30, 2011] used his health care law to hand a lucrative special favor to two industries that have ardently supported his party: Planned Parenthood and the drug industry.

The largesse came in the form of a rule proposed by the Department of Health and Human Services [HHS] that would require all new insurance plans to cover the entire cost of all forms of prescription contraception—including those that also act as abortion drugs.

This free-pills-for-all proposal embodies two dark themes of the Obama era: cronyism and trampling on the freedom of conscience.

A Gift for Special-Interest Groups

Once again, Obama, who pretends to be battling the special interests, is rewarding powerful lobbies that support him. Even worse, the federal rule, which would effectively force everyone to purchase insurance that covers abortifacient [drugs that cause abortion] contraceptives, also reveals the true shape of the Culture War in America: The Left uses the brutal tool of the government to impose its morality on everyone, forcing religious conservatives to act against conscience, all the while howling about imminent "theocracy."

Pharmaceuticals are the quintessential "special interest." Drugmakers have spent $2.2 billion on lobbying since 1998, according to the Center for Responsive Politics, more than any other industry. In the Obama era, the drug industry's $635 million lobbying tab exceeds that of Wall Street and the oil and gas industry, combined.

For the 2010 election, as a reward for passing Obamacare, Big Pharma spent millions in ads boosting vulnerable Democratic senators including Harry Reid. Obamacare subsidized the drug companies in many ways, but it's hard to get better than this "free contraception" rule. Obamacare requires individuals to carry insurance and forces large employers to insure their workers. It also prohibits insurance companies from turning down applicants, and subsidizes more people's insurance.

Finally, Obamacare will force all insurers to fully cover all prescription contraceptives and not charge a co-pay. So everyone has to buy insurance, and everyone's insurance has to cover contraception. Government has become a magical money machine for drugmakers.

The Triumph of Planned Parenthood

Planned Parenthood, intimately tied to the Democratic Party's money machine, is another prime beneficiary of Obama's proposed rule. Planned Parenthood has in the past set up special profitable arrangements with drugmakers such as Barr Pharmaceuticals, which sold the Plan B [emergency contraceptive] morning-after pill (an abortifacient).

HHS Secretary Kathleen Sebelius has a long and lucrative relationship with the drug industry. As governor of Kansas, she supported subsidies for embryo research and, in turn, received more than $400,000 in backing from a biotech industry group.

But more troubling than the special-interest collusion with government is the assault on economic freedom and freedom of conscience.

> ## The History of Birth Control Coverage
>
> As recently as the 1990s, many health insurance plans didn't even cover birth control. Protests, court cases, and new state laws led to dramatic changes. Today, almost all plans cover prescription contraceptives—with varying co-pays.
>
> *Ricardo Alonso-Zaldivar,*
> *"Insurers to Cover Birth Control,"*
> Associated Press, *August 1, 2011.*

The Role of Morality and Conscience

The rule would force folks who don't want contraception insurance to pay for contraception. Acting of their own free will, infertile couples, gay people, celibate people or post-menopausal women would not buy contraception insurance. Obama's mandate—like similar mandates in 28 states—unnecessarily drives up these people's health insurance.

But with prescription contraception, conscience enters the picture.

First, there is the (admittedly small) minority of observant Catholics who follow Rome's teaching that contraception subverts the procreative nature of marital sex. While most health care plans cover contraception, Obamacare's rules and proposed rules would basically make it illegal for someone to not pay for contraception.

Emergency Contraception

But the proposed rule, promulgated under Obamacare's mandate for "free" preventive care, doesn't just cover the Pill, it also covers "morning-after" contraceptives that sometimes work by killing a fertilized egg that has already begun cell division. In other words, these are also abortion pills.

Plan B's manufacturers admitted the drug could "prevent pregnancy" by stopping a zygote from implanting on its mother's uterus (once implanted, the zygote is called an embryo).

The new "morning-after" pill being promoted by Planned Parenthood, called "ella" is closer to the avowed abortion pill, RU-486, than to Plan B. While ella can delay ovulation, and thus prevent fertilization, it also can prevent a zygote from implanting, or—to use the FDA's word—"affect" implantation. What does that mean? "Ella starves an implanted embryo to death," Anna Franzonello, attorney for Americans United for Life, tells me. The drug, like RU-486, blocks progesterone, the chemical the uterus needs in order to host an embryo.

Unsatisfactory Religious Exemptions

The administration's proposed rule has a conscience exception for religious institutions, but "religious institution" is defined so narrowly that it wouldn't include a Catholic school—though a seminary would probably be protected.

Still, Planned Parenthood and NARAL Pro-Choice America are lobbying to kill even this conscience protection—gotta make sure those Catholic priests-in-training don't have to pay $25 for their ella!

The intersection of pharma and government is full of Orwellian Newspeak. Drugmakers say they're preventing pregnancies by ending them. Obama claims he's depoliticizing science by increasing subsidies and regulations. Then he crows about fighting special interests in the act of rewarding them.

Most bizarrely, the cultural Left assails "culture warriors" while making it illegal for many cultural conservatives to live according to their conscience.

> *"The government should not be telling religious organizations that to be true to themselves, they must keep to themselves."*

The Religious Exemptions for Universal Birth Control Coverage Should Be Broader

Hannah C. Smith

Hannah C. Smith is a member of the Deseret News *Editorial Advisory Board and senior counsel at the Becket Fund for Religious Liberty. In the following viewpoint, she contends that the new Department of Health and Human Services (HHS) regulations that mandate insurance companies to cover prescribed contraceptive methods is repugnant to many people of religious faith. Although there is a religious exemption provided by HHS that allows religious employers to opt out of the new policy, Smith argues that it is too narrow and will leave out many religious institutions, such as Catholic hospitals and colleges, because they do not serve primarily one religious faith. She states that it is wrong for the government to dictate to such institutions just because they minister to people of all faiths.*

As you read, consider the following questions:

1. According to the author, when were the new HHS regulations put in place?

2. What did the Heritage Foundation conclude about the new HHS regulations, according to the author?

3. Why does the author say non-Catholics should be alarmed by the government's actions?

Last week [July 31–August 6, 2011] the U.S. Department of Health and Human Services [HHS] issued new federal regulations that run roughshod over the moral conscience of many Americans.

Promulgated under the health care reform act commonly referred to as "Obamacare," the new regulations would require an employer to have a health plan that covers sterilization and contraception—which could include drugs that cause abortion—as part of a larger set of "preventative services" for women. These practices are morally repugnant to many Americans—for some, because it directly contradicts their faith. For example, the doctrine of the [Roman] Catholic Church, which includes roughly a quarter of Americans, explicitly prohibits such practices.

HHS, apparently recognizing the regulations' tension with religious belief, did include an exemption from the new regulations for a "religious employer." But close examination reveals that the exemption may actually cover very few religious employers. So the rule may force out of existence those social service and educational organizations that are the core manifestations of the Catholic doctrine to serve the poor and needy among us.

Indeed, the exemption defines a religious employer as a nonprofit that inculcates religious values "as its purpose" and which primarily employs and serves those who share its faith. Many Catholic organizations—including schools, colleges, hospitals, and charitable organizations—could fail to meet this definition. Those organizations could be forced to choose between covering drugs, devices, and procedures contrary to church doctrine or closing their doors.

A Premeditated Attack

Why the exemption was drawn so narrowly is puzzling. An analysis by the Heritage Foundation finds that "the only reasonable conclusion is that the [Barack] Obama administration has purposefully targeted personal and institutional conscience on morally controversial issues such as sterilization, contraception and abortifacients."

It further concludes that "it is impossible to view the new guideline as anything less than a premeditated squeeze on conscience"—squeezed because being too religious or not religious enough are both penalized.

In many cases, to receive federal funds a social service organization must certify that it provides that service without regard to the religious belief of the recipients. But to qualify for the exemption from the new regulations, a religious employer must "primarily serve persons who share its religious tenets."

The implication is clear. These religious organizations must now choose between their ministry and beliefs. Whatever the reason for designing the exemption so narrowly, the effect reinforces an ominous recent trend: seeking to sequester religious organizations from American public life.

A Backlash Against the New Policy

It's easy to see that Catholics care about the false choice these regulations impose—and to see why they do. This week, Catholic commentators have filled the blogosphere exposing this aggressive attack on their deeply held religious beliefs. The Catholic belief in the sanctity of life and the respect for the union that produces life compels its opposition to contraception and sterilization.

At the same time, the Biblical command to serve the poor and needy, including those of other faiths, motivates Catholic organizations' ministering to those most vulnerable in our society. Across the country, Catholic organizations minister in homeless shelters, adoption service centers, women's shelters, pregnancy support service centers, shelters for troubled teens, schools that serve disadvantaged youths, and hospitals that care for Catholics and non-Catholics alike.

Why should non-Catholics care? Why should these regulations bother the conscience of those whose religious beliefs do not disavow contraception or sterilization?

The Role of Government

The government should not force out of civil society those religious organizations that meaningfully engage or minister to those of other faiths or no faith. The troubling message conveyed by the government's action here is that the government approves of religious organizations keeping to themselves in their ministry. But once those organizations choose to serve anyone else, the government can dictate which doctrines can be honored in that ministry and which must be abandoned.

All those who are motivated by religious belief to serve their communities have a strong interest in Catholic organizations' ability to minister while remaining true to their doctrines. The community ministries of various churches tend to complement each other's efforts, with each religious organization reaching some people that others miss.

Our constitutional democracy contemplates restraining our government and enabling a robust civil society including religious organizations that provide a social safety net for those of any faith or no faith. These new regulations reverse that structure. They constrain a key contributor to our civil society while enabling the government to force religious organizations into an unnecessary and false choice.

The government should not be telling religious organizations that to be true to themselves, they must keep to themselves.

VIEWPOINT

"Religious adherents who object to a particular medical service are under no obligation to use it."

There Should Not Be a Religious Exemption for Universal Birth Control Coverage

Nancy Northup

Nancy Northup is president and chief executive officer of the Center for Reproductive Rights. In the following viewpoint, she suggests that religious exemptions that allow religious institutions to opt out of insurance coverage they do not agree with, like contraception, would allow any insurer to claim certain medical services that they do not like go against their religious beliefs. Northup argues the United States cannot allow religious dogma to influence sound public health policy. Since birth control is an essential service that the overwhelming majority of American women use and support, she contends, it should be covered without religious exemptions.

As you read, consider the following questions:

1. What did Jeffrey Kuhner of the *Washington Times* write about the new Department of Health and Human Services regulations on birth control coverage, according to the viewpoint?

2. What percentage of American women have used birth control, according to the author?

3. According to the author, what percentage of American pregnancies are unplanned?

When the Institute of Medicine's [IOM] independent panel of health experts recommended last week [July 24–30, 2011] that insurers offer preventive services to women without co-payments, the reaction was swift. Despite IOM's reliance on medical science, its recommendation on contraception, in particular, was greeted with howls of disapproval.

Some of the right wing's ravings have been positively unhinged. Jeffrey Kuhner of the *Washington Times* wrote that contraception "violates the natural moral order" and that the recommendation on birth control is a step toward "forging a pagan society based on consequence-free sex." Fox host Bill O'Reilly claimed the recommendation would be ineffective because "many women who get pregnant are blasted out of their minds when they have sex and [are] not going to use birth control anyway." Fox's Greg Gutfield, bizarrely, argued that eliminating co-pays would help so many low-income women that it must be part of a plot to "eradicate the poor."

The Widespread Popularity of Birth Control

To listen to the hysteria, you would think that coverage for birth control is divisive. It's not. Most plans already cover it, and a majority of states—28, to be precise—require it be covered by insurance. Virtually all women—99%—have used

Letter from the United States Conference of Catholic Bishops (USCCB) to the US Department of Health and Human Services (HHS)

In sum, we urge HHS to rescind the mandate in its entirety. Only rescission will eliminate all of the serious moral problems the mandate creates; only rescission will correct HHS's legally flawed interpretation of the term "preventive services." If HHS nonetheless persists in mandating coverage of contraceptives, sterilization, and related education and counseling, it must address the especially grave legal and constitutional problems it creates (1) by including in the mandate those drugs that can cause an abortion, and (2) by failing to protect all stakeholders with a religious or moral objection to the mandate. HHS is legally forbidden from mandating coverage of any drug that can cause an abortion, and from forcing individuals or institutions to provide coverage for contraception, sterilization, or related education and counseling over their religious or moral objections.

Indeed, such nationwide government coercion of religious people and groups to sell, broker, or purchase "services" to which they have a moral or religious objection represents an unprecedented attack on religious liberty.

United States Conference of Catholic Bishops letter to the US Department of Health and Human Services, August 31, 2011.

birth control, and religious adherents, even Catholics and Evangelicals, use birth control at the same rate as the general population. (Ninety-eight percent of sexually active Catholic women have used birth control; the rate is even higher among

Evangelicals.) In addition, government insurance plans currently cover contraception, albeit with co-pays.

This near-universal acceptance of contraception is remarkable. In this age of red and blue states, we may not agree on politics, or even basic scientific truths: half of Americans don't believe in evolution, and one in three Americans believes in ghosts. Yet Americans are united in their acceptance of birth control, making it as mainstream as anything could be.

Access to Contraception in the United States

At the same time, access to affordable contraception is lacking. The U.S. leads the developed world in unintended pregnancies—a shocking half of all American pregnancies are unplanned. Unintended pregnancy can harm women's health, and closely spaced pregnancies are associated with low birth weight and prematurity. Cost, sadly, has been the major factor preventing the more widespread use of birth control, particularly in an economic downturn. Moreover, the high cost of long-acting contraceptive options like IUDs places them out of reach for millions, leading to contraceptive failure when antibiotics or mere forgetfulness renders birth control pills less effective. The IOM's recommendation to eliminate co-pays for the "full range" of approved contraceptives was grounded in two facts: contraception is non-controversial and has been used by virtually every American woman; and women lack access to affordable contraception.

Yet this commonsense, evidence-based approach is under attack. Not only by the hyperbolic antics of television's talking heads, but also the misleading statements of the U.S. Conference of Catholic Bishops. Its public statements repeatedly and deliberately conflate contraception with abortion, which is beyond the scope of IOM's recommendations.

A Vocal Minority

The all-male minority and avowed celibate Bishops want a heckler's veto over the entire American health care system, including preventive services for women. Sister Mary Ann Walsh, a spokeswoman, has argued for an exception to allow religious insurers to operate under a different, special set of rules. Never mind that Catholics need and use birth control just like everyone else, and that a special rule for some insurers would deny coverage to many non-believers who happen to work for religiously affiliated hospitals or schools.

When considering religious prohibitions that she does not share, Walsh gets the distinction between what an individual chooses to use under a plan and forcing everyone to forgo it. In the *Washington Post's On Faith* blog, she notes that "[b]lood transfusions are not verboten to me, but I respect Jehovah's Witnesses' right to refuse them." The obvious rejoinder, then, is that for the rest of us, "contraceptives are not verboten to us, but we respect Catholics' right to refuse them." Religious adherents who object to a particular medical service are under no obligation to use it. Jehovah's Witnesses are not compelled to get blood transfusions, and Catholics are not compelled to use contraceptives.

The Weapon of Religious Dogma

Respect for others' choices isn't what Walsh and the Bishops want. Instead, they seek a rule that would allow any insurer allied with a set of religious beliefs to deny coverage to everyone they insure. Under this dubious logic, the government couldn't mandate coverage for any medical service that anyone had a religious objection to, allowing religious dogma to trump sound public health policy.

The purpose of health care reform is to make needed medical care practically available and uniform for a much larger group of people, thereby improving health and diminishing costs. (The IOM focused on health, but noted cost savings would be $19 billion). The IOM's recommendations are a critical step to improve the health of millions. Birth control should finally take its rightful place as an essential medical service. It is medically sound, cost effective, and uncontroversial. Any set of special rules that would reduce access for some would merely diminish the quality of care for everyone.

"America has a long tradition of legally recognizing objections of conscience."

Pharmacists Should Have the Right to Refuse to Dispense Birth Control

Joel Connelly

Joel Connelly is a staff writer for the Seattle Post-Intelligencer. *In the following viewpoint, he applauds a proposed compromise in the state of Washington that would allow pharmacists to refuse to dispense prescriptions to which they morally object, such as birth control or emergency contraception. Connelly criticizes the rigid opposition to the compromise by progressive activists, finding it hypocritical that they do not support a person's right to follow his or her own conscience on matters of faith. He points out that the United States has a long history of objections of conscience, and this should be considered within that storied tradition.*

As you read, consider the following questions:

1. What did the 9th Circuit Court of Appeals rule on the issue of Washington's law on dispensing medication, according to the viewpoint?

2. According to the author, what did Governor Chris Gregoire say about the proposed compromise to the law?

3. Who does the author describe as "zealous advocates" who have framed the issue in Washington State?

Compromise is a curse word, and conscience a concept often dismissed, to posturing combatants in the never-ending battle between pro-choice and pro-life forces.

Naturally, talk of settlement and accommodation in a federal lawsuit over whether pharmacists can refuse to provide certain medications—even if a referral is available—is drawing fire.

It is a case that puts rights in conflict.

"No one should be able to impose their personal beliefs on a woman seeking birth control, or on anyone seeking safe lawful medications," NARAL Pro-Choice Washington thundered in a fund-raising appeal last month.

The case, facing trial in the Tacoma courtroom of U.S. District Judge Ronald Leighton, is a challenge by two pharmacists and an Olympia pharmacy to a Washington State Board of Pharmacy rule requiring all licensed pharmacies to fill patients' prescriptions with no dissent or delay, whatever the individual pharmacist's personal beliefs about the medication being prescribed.

Last month, plaintiffs and the state joined in a motion to stay the trial. The stay anticipated a change in which the Board of Pharmacy would slightly relax the existing rule.

Under a revised rule, pharmacists and pharmacies that oppose on conscience a patient's prescriptions would be permitted to decline service and refer the patient to a different pharmacy.

The U.S. 9th Circuit Court of Appeals has already been heard, finding that the "(Board of Pharmacy) rules do not aim to suppress, target or single out in any way the practice of religion but, rather, their objective was to increase access to all lawfully prescribed medications."

Seattlepi.com asked Gov. Chris Gregoire about the proposed accommodation. She does not like it. Gregoire is a Catholic, but has been a strong advocate of the current rule and a supporter of abortion rights.

"I've had no contact with the (pharmacy) board," the governor said. "I'm disappointed they've chosen this route ... I think we are on the path to winning (the lawsuit)."

Gregoire intends to speak to the Board of Pharmacy. "This better be an open, transparent process and not a predetermined process," she said. Would pharmacists be able to deny AIDS drugs, or even anti-smoking remedies? asked Gregoire.

Nor is Gregoire satisfied with the referral solution. "You refer me and I am in rural Eastern Washington: You expect me to drive 60 or 70 miles to get the prescription. It's unfair."

Of course, there is another side to the case.

America has a long tradition of legally recognizing objections of conscience. We've allowed pacifists to opt out of military service and provided for alternative service. We, as a society, have also sanctioned the primacy of free speech. Civil disobedience has left a positive mark, e.g. the 1960s' civil rights movement.

Are these traditions being jeopardized by zealous advocates—e.g. NARAL Pro-Choice Washington and Planned Parenthood Votes! (PPV)—who cast conscientious objection as trumping patients' rights?

"Like all true tragedy, it is a conflict between valid rights but in this case (rule supporters) make no allowance for compromise," said Chris Carlson. Carlson is a Spokane businessman, cancer survivor, Gregoire supporter and opponent of the initiative that legalized assisted suicide in Washington.

"They want a pharmacist forced to provide Plan B's morning-after pill and if a pharmacist can't in good con-

> ## Pharmacists Have a Long History of Objecting to Dispensing the Pill
>
> Since the introduction of oral contraceptives (the pill) in 1964, a quiet battle has been waged to prohibit women from obtaining the pill. The most vocal opponents of the pill are those who believe it to be the roots of the breakdown of traditional family values, and those who believe any manipulation of a woman's fertility is a "sin against God," and therefore immoral. The latter viewpoint has prompted a growing number of pharmacists to claim a "conscientious objector" status toward dispensing products such as birth control pills and emergency contraception.
>
> *Jen, "Conscientious Objection:*
> *Not Just for the Military Anymore,"* BrooWaha,
> *June 30, 2007. www.broowaha.com.*

science do so, their attitude is the state should strip this person of license and livelihood," he added.

Another question: Is the Board of Pharmacy rule a "slippery slope" which could trump a medical professional's right to opt out of such objectionable procedures as providing the lethal "cocktail" of drugs that allows terminally ill patients to kill themselves?

Ours is a complex society. Sometimes its rule makers are moved to fashion compromise solutions, seeking to avoid disharmony and confontation—angering those who use confrontation to raise money.

"We know that a strong majority of Washingtonians, from Seattle to Spokane, from Bellingham to Vancouver, support access to medications like emergency contraception (also known as the morning-after pill) at the pharmacy counter," NARAL argued in its appeal for dollars.

Oh, to be so certain and so stigmatize those who disagree. Again, however, a broader question: Should everyone be forced to acquiesce to a majority view, even if the majority is slim or conflicted?

Progressive activists in Washington are longtime champions of conscience, defending service personnel who refused to serve in Vietnam and Iraq, and the first pre-1970 public provider—Dr. Koome—who performed abortions when it was against the law.

In the case of *Stormans et al. v Selecky et. al.*, however, people acting out of deep personal belief are, in the words of Elaine Rose, CEO of Planned Parenthood Votes! Washington, "a few extremist pharmacists who are putting their personal beliefs before their patients' health care."

Should we recognize claims of conscience only when we agree with the objectors, while stigmatizing and sneering at others? I'd like to see a little liberal tolerance.

> *"Professionals should be able to make moral stands in defiance of their official duties* only *if they are willing to take the heat afterwards, and pay the price."*

Pharmacists Should Not Be Able to Refuse to Dispense Birth Control

Jack Marshall

Jack Marshall is an ethicist and a lawyer. In the following viewpoint, he describes conscience clauses—exemptions from regulations that allow pharmacists to refuse to dispense controversial drugs like birth control—as unethical. Marshall argues that if pharmacists or other health professionals feel so strongly about an issue, they should take a stand and then face the consequences of their actions. Codifying a conscience clause into law should not be permitted, he contends, because society would then be subjected to all sorts of objections and refusals for a number of moral, cultural, and religious reasons.

As you read, consider the following questions:

1. According to the author, when did conscience clauses originate?

2. Are US soldiers permitted to refuse to obey an illegal order, according to Marshall?

3. What is one of Marshall's examples of what could happen if we allowed conscience clauses?

The [Barack] Obama administration has deep-sixed a controversial [George W.] Bush administration rule that permitted a wide variety of health care workers to refuse to administer treatments they found morally repugnant, what the Bush administration termed workers' "right of conscience."

Hospitals and clinics faced a loss of federal funds if they failed to uphold the rule, which itself was ethically repugnant. Kudos, thanks and hosannas to President Obama for getting rid of the federal variety; some states, regrettably, still have them.

The AMA's Position on the Conscience Clause

The American Medical Association's [AMA's] position on the matter, embodied in a resolution passed by its membership, is clear and well reasoned. Its reasoning applies to health care workers though the specific subject of the resolution was pharmacist conscience clauses.

The AMA's resolution, "Preserving Patients' Ability To Have Legally Valid Prescriptions Filled," states:

> "RESOLVED, That our American Medical Association reaffirm our policies supporting responsibility to the patient as paramount in all situations and the principle of access to medical care for all people (Reaffirm HOD Policy); and be it further.

RESOLVED, That our AMA support legislation that requires individual pharmacists or pharmacy chains to fill legally valid prescriptions or to provide immediate referral to an appropriate alternative dispensing pharmacy without interference (New HOD Policy); and be it further.

"RESOLVED, That our AMA work with state medical societies to support legislation to protect patients' ability to have legally valid prescriptions filled.

"RESOLVED, That our AMA enter into discussions with relevant associations (including but not limited to the American Hospital Association, American Pharmacists Association, American Society of Health System Pharmacists, National Association of Chain Drug Stores, and National Community Pharmacists Association) to guarantee that, if an individual pharmacist exercises a conscientious refusal to dispense a legal prescription, a patient's right to obtain legal prescriptions will be protected by immediate referral to an appropriate dispensing pharmacy.

"RESOLVED, That our AMA, in the absence of all other remedies, work with state medical societies to adopt state legislation that will allow physicians to dispense medication to their own patients when there is no pharmacist within a thirty-mile radius who is able and willing to dispense that medication."

I wrote about conscience clauses when they were raising their ugly heads with increasing frequency back in 2005, primarily in relation to pharmacists refusing to help single women obtain birth control. The news that the Bush rule had been sent to Ethics Hell where it belongs caused me to re-read the post, and my assessment of their unethical nature hasn't changed one iota since I wrote it (though the version below has been lightly re-edited):

A Wisconsin pharmacist named Neil Noesen refused to fill University of Wisconsin student Amanda Phiede's birth control prescription on religious grounds, and now faces discipline from the state Pharmacy Examination Board. He also managed to call attention to a growing call for so-called "conscience clauses" in state laws that would permit pharmacists to withhold professional services that they found morally objectionable.

Conscience Clauses

"Conscience clauses" came into being in the wake of the Supreme Court's *Roe v. Wade* opinion legalizing abortion. Obviously that right to privacy ruling put Catholic hospitals in a difficult position, so the U.S. Congress passed the Church amendment (named after Sen. Frank Church of Idaho) in 1973. This provision allowed individual health care providers and institutions such as hospitals to refuse to provide abortion and sterilization services, based on moral or religious convictions. Most states adopted their own "conscience clause" laws by 1978.

. . . Conscience clauses are a terrible idea that encourage arbitrary professional misconduct. It is an example of how morally based action can lead to unethical conduct.

An especially wrongheaded "commentary" that appeared a while back in the *Los Angeles Times* argued otherwise. In it, Crispin Sartwell, who teaches political philosophy at Dickinson College in Carlisle, Pa., stated his opinion that:

> ". . . I personally am no opponent of birth control of any sort or, for that matter, of abortion rights. But people whose jobs require them to violate their own deeply held convictions ought to refuse to do the job, and any politician who upholds freedom or dignity must uphold their right to do so.

> "What you should ask yourself in this case is not whether you think people should have access to birth control, but

The American Public Opposes Pharmacy Refusals to Fill Birth Control Prescriptions

According to surveys, the public is overwhelmingly opposed to allowing refusals in the pharmacy that prevent women from obtaining contraception.

- A national survey of Republicans and Independent voters conducted in September and October 2008 on behalf of the National Women's Law Center and the YWCA found that 51% strongly favor legislation that requires pharmacies to ensure that patients get contraception at their pharmacy of choice, even if a particular pharmacist has a moral objection to contraceptives and refuses to provide it. That includes 42% of Republicans and 62% of Independents.

"Pharmacy Refusals 101,"
National Women's Law Center, July 2011.

whether you should be required to do things that violate your deepest convictions. Should a soldier be required to torture prisoners, for example? Should he refuse to do so if ordered? Should a liberal corporate peon be required to contribute to the Republican Party? Should a Christian secretary have to assist in the advocacy of man-boy love?"

Well, Professor Sartwell, since you ask. . .yes, *people who voluntarily undertake the duties of a job should either be prepared to fulfill those duties, take the consequences of not doing so, or not take the job in the first place.*

That is the ethical duty that one accepts when one agrees to do a job. This couldn't be clearer.

Examples of Conscience

Sartwell's examples are terrible:

- U.S. soldiers are, in fact, not only permitted to refuse to obey an illegal order (like being ordered to torture a prisoner) but are *required* to do so.

- Contributing to a political party is not a duty of employment, and refusing to obey an order to do so has nothing to do with "conscience."

- His last bizarre example comes from the beginning of his essay, in which he describes a supposedly true anecdote about a devoutly religious woman who served as a secretary for an executive who had her type letters related to his involvement in the National Man-Boy Love Association [NAMBLA]. She needed the job, you see, but didn't feel it was right to type his letters. But she didn't, in Sartwell's terms, "have to assist in the advocacy of man-boy love." Nowhere are typists regarded as active participants in the projects related to the letters they type; it is not as if the letter wasn't going to be typed if she didn't do it. But more importantly, she didn't have to type the letter at all. She just had to type it if she wanted to keep her job. His argument here is like saying an actor can refuse to speak lines he doesn't agree with, and still play the role he was cast in.

This calls to mind a court case of a few years back in which a National Basketball Association player was suspended for refusing to stand when the National Anthem was played before games. He said his religion prohibited doing so, and sued. The NBA pointed out that the standard player contract requires players to follow such team rituals. That was enough for the court, which ruled that the player was free to exercise his conscience, but not if he wanted to continue to play in the NBA.

The call for conscience clauses is just another chapter in what I sometimes refer to as the ethical "weeny-fication" of America, in which advocates strive assiduously to take all risk, danger and courage out of moral stands. Courage is a great and necessary test of conviction, and it must not be removed from ethical decision making. Professionals should be able to make moral stands in defiance of their official duties *only if they are willing to take the heat afterwards, and pay the price.*

Taking a Stand Should Have Consequences

Without this necessary feature, we would all be subjected to paralyzing refusals to fulfill basic duties for moral reasons large, small, eccentric and imaginary. The PETA [People for the Ethical Treatment of Animals] member check-out clerk who won't allow you to buy steak and eggs; the ecologically minded Home Depot worker who refuses to let you buy pesticide for your peach trees; the religiously teetotalling bar waitress who will only serve you soft drinks; the SUV-hating gas station attendant who won't let a gas-guzzling, global-warming Ford Suburban fill up; the Democrat-detesting poll worker who won't let one of those socialist Obama-lovers vote; the Fundamentalist science teacher who refuses to teach Bible-denying evolution ... oh, one can come up with endless examples, and, frankly, none are any more absurd than the pharmacist that began this discussion.

He has no professional right to refuse to fill a lawful prescription directed by a physician. He has no right at all to make his customer feel like she is doing something wrong, or to inconvenience her by making her go to another store, which might be miles and miles away. His job is to fill prescriptions, not judge them, and if he cannot do that, he shouldn't be a pharmacist.

Conscience Clauses

He is free to make his stand, and indeed, there are times a stand is appropriate ... but it is extremely unwise to pass laws to make moral stands widespread and without consequences.

Do I want surgeons free to refuse to operate on criminals, child molesters, adulterers, drug pushers, Michael Moore, Tom DeLay, Paris Hilton, Professor Sartwell's friend's NAMBLA boss or Howard Stern just because [the surgeons] may be morally certain that the world would be better off without [such individuals]? No, I don't, and neither do you. And, I suspect, neither would Professor Sartwell, if he gave the issue just a bit more thought.

"If you claim the right to behave in accordance with your conscience," he writes at the end of his article, "then you also must accord that right to all others, even pharmacists."

Perhaps. But you do not have the right to avoid all consequences that flow from your exercise of that "right." You have to have the courage to go along with the moral stand, the guts to risk the consequences. The NBA player can refuse to stand for the National Anthem, if he's willing to pick cherries for a living. Neil Noesen can refuse to fill the prescription, if he's game for employment at Blockbuster.

Periodical and Internet Sources Bibliography

The following articles have been selected to supplement the diverse views presented in this chapter.

Vanessa Cullins	"Why Birth Control with No Co-Pay Will Help African-American Women," *Huffington Post*, August 4, 2011. www.huffingtonpost.com.
Chuck Donovan	"Mandating Coverage of Contraceptives Is Bad Social Policy," *The Foundry*, July 25, 2011. http://blog.heritage.org.
David Gibson	"Religious Groups Irked by Contraception Mandate," *National Catholic Reporter*, August 16, 2011.
Jenn Giroux	"Government Mandated Birth Control Coverage: Placing Women at Higher Risk for Cancer and Catholic Hospitals at Risk of Closing," Renew America, August 2, 2011. www.renewamerica.com.
Star Parker	"New Obamacare Violations of Personal Liberty," Townhall.com, August 8, 2011.
Lucia Rafanelli	"Birth Control for All?," *American Spectator*, July 28, 2011.
Cecile Richards	"Birth Control You Can Afford—It's About Time!," *Huffington Post*, August 3, 2011. www.huffingtonpost.com.
Annamarya Scaccia	"Religious Exemptions and Contraceptive Coverage: How Far Can Denial Go and Still Be Constitutional?," RH Reality Check, September 30, 2011. www.rhrealitycheck.org.
StarTribune (Minneapolis)	"Benefits Outweigh Birth Control Costs," July 31, 2011.

OPPOSING
VIEWPOINTS®
SERIES

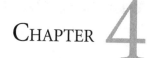

CHAPTER 4

What Is the Best Approach to Birth Control and Sex Education for Teens?

Chapter Preface

When it comes to sex education in America, abstinence-only education has played a prominent role for the past thirty years. Abstinence-only education accurately teaches that abstinence is the only way to avoid both unplanned pregnancy and sexually transmitted diseases and recommends that young people refrain from having sex until they are married. It excludes more comprehensive teaching on birth control, such as family planning and safe sex information.

The rise of abstinence-only education in contemporary education programs can be traced back to the Adolescent Family Life Act (AFLA), a 1981 law that created "family-centered" programs to encourage abstinence and self-discipline. The ultimate goal of the AFLA was to reduce the number of teen pregnancies in the United States. It also set out to encourage adoption instead of abortion for teens faced with an unplanned pregnancy. Supporters of the AFLA argued that family planning programs at the time put too much emphasis on contraception and not enough on abstinence as a way to avoid teen pregnancy.

Some of the AFLA funding ended up going to conservative religious groups that promoted religious teaching. In 1983 the American Civil Liberties Union (ACLU) filed a lawsuit against the AFLA, arguing that it promoted religion and violated the separation between church and state. The case took years to adjudicate; finally, in 1993, an agreement was reached that organizations and institutions receiving AFLA funds must submit to a review by the US Department of Health and Human Services (HHS).

The enactment of welfare reform in 1996 led to the allocation of $50 million dollars a year to fund abstinence-only programs. It also established an eight-point definition of abstinence-only education. According to the United States Social Security Act, an eligible abstinence education program is one that does the following:

(A) has as its exclusive purpose, teaching the social, psychological, and health gains to be realized by abstaining from sexual activity;

(B) teaches abstinence from sexual activity outside marriage as the expected standard for all school-age children;

(C) teaches that abstinence from sexual activity is the only certain way to avoid out-of-wedlock pregnancy, sexually transmitted diseases, and other associated health problems;

(D) teaches that a mutually faithful monogamous relationship in the context of marriage is the expected standard of human sexual activity;

(E) teaches that sexual activity outside of the context of marriage is likely to have harmful psychological and physical effects;

(F) teaches that bearing children out of wedlock is likely to have harmful consequences for the child, the child's parents, and society;

(G) teaches young people how to reject sexual advances and how alcohol and drug use increases vulnerability to sexual advances; and

(H) teaches the importance of attaining self-sufficiency before engaging in sexual activity.[1]

In 2000 the Special Projects of Regional and National Significance Community-Based Abstinence Education Program (now known as CBAE) was established by the U.S. Congress. To receive funds from the CBAE, organizations were required to fulfill all eight principles of federal eligibility. In 2007 Congress allocated $113 million for the CBAE to fund abstinence-only education programs.

Under the administration of President Barack Obama, funding for abstinence-only education programs began to decline. In the president's 2009 budget, he shifted funding from abstinence-only programs to teen pregnancy programs that emphasize comprehensive sex education and information on safe sex.

The efficacy of abstinence-only and comprehensive sex education is one of the topics explored in the following chapter, which examines the best approaches to birth control and sex education for teens. Other viewpoints in the chapter discuss teen access to emergency contraception and providing condoms in schools.

Notes

1. U.S. Social Security Administration, Compilation of the Social Security Laws, "Separate Program for Abstinence Education," Social Security Act, Sec. 510. [42 U.S.C. 710], 2011. www.ssa.gov.

| *"Teen girls say they want to hear the abstinence message."*

Teens Should Be Encouraged to Practice Abstinence

Jennifer Marshall

Jennifer Marshall is an author and director of the DeVos Center for Religion and Civil Society at The Heritage Foundation. In the following viewpoint, she points out that many young women have been negatively affected by the culture of casual sex that pervades society today. Marshall argues that we should be providing abstinence education for young women, which gives them the tools to avoid sexually transmitted diseases and the depression and regret that come from casual sexual encounters. She states that abstinence education will empower young women to navigate a confusing sexual landscape and make the right choices for their future.

As you read, consider the following questions:

1. According to the author, what percentage of young women say they truly wanted to have sex the first time they did?

2. According to the author, what percentage of sexually active girls is less likely to go to college than their abstaining peers?

3. How much less likely were middle school students to engage in sexual activity after eight hours of abstinence education, according to Marshall?

A group that thinks a Super Bowl ad celebrating Tim Tebow's life is bad news for women might be a little out of touch with what women really want.

That helps explain why the National Organization for Women and other feminist groups have vehemently opposed abstinence education while failing to notice that a culture of casual sex hasn't been so liberating for women.

The Problem with Casual Sex

Just ask the 29-year-old Briton living in America whose anonymous account appeared in her country's left-wing *Guardian* newspaper.

"(M)y sexual liberation was perversely trapping me in destructive relationships, while intimacy had become something elusive, insubstantial, disappointing, surreal," she writes.

Weary of a "burlesque comedy where we all pretended we were emotionless and cool," she decided to stop having sex because "I wanted sex to be, quite simply, special again."

Similar world-weary statements have been recorded by researchers such as Dr. Miriam Grossman, author of *Unprotected*, and Laura Sessions Stepp, author of *Unhooked: How Young Women Pursue Sex, Delay Love and Lose at Both.*

A Confusing Sexual Landscape

Only a third of young women say they truly wanted to have sex the first time they did, Stepp reports. Young women, she writes, "are trying to make sense of what is arguably the most confusing sexual landscape any generation has ever faced."

Most sex education pushes young women into this jungle and tells them contraception will provide adequate protection. This puts incredible pressure on those who have the most at risk in the casual-sex scene. And it jeopardizes their dreams of long-term security and love.

The vast majority of young women say marriage and motherhood are important to future happiness. Why wouldn't we equip young women to achieve those dreams while avoiding such consequences as sexual assault and serious disease—to say nothing of bewildering heartache? Why not teach young women the real facts about the risks of early sexual activity?

Teen girls who engage in sex are more vulnerable to sexually transmitted disease and depression. Girls who are sexually active in high school are half as likely to go on to college as abstaining peers from the same social setting. Later, they often have more difficulty in forging the kind of lasting relationships that lead to marriage.

Giving Women the Right Foundation

Why not help young women make social choices that advance their long-term educational, vocational and marriage prospects? What about teaching tactics for resisting unwanted sexual advances? How about helping girls build relational and communication skills that will allow them to get what they really want—lasting love?

This commonsense approach is exactly what abstinence education seeks to do. Contrary to its detractors' caricature, abstinence education aims to empower young people—especially young women—with the information, skills and long-term perspective they need to successfully navigate what Stepp calls today's "confusing sexual landscape."

Evidence Supporting Abstinence Education

New evidence says this approach is helping girls do exactly that.

The Efficacy of Abstinence-Only Sex Education

A 2010 study in the medical journal *Archives of Pediatrics & Adolescent Medicine*, published by the American Medical Association, concludes that an "abstinence-only intervention reduced sexual initiation" as well as recent sexual activity among a group of African American adolescents. Two years after attending an eight-hour abstinence program, about one-third of the participants had initiated sexual activity, compared to nearly one-half of the non-participants who enrolled in a general health program. That is, the abstinence program reduced the rate of sexual initiation by one-third. Moreover, abstinence program participants who became sexually active were not less likely to use contraception.

By contrast, the study also evaluated two alternative interventions, one that only taught contraception (i.e., the "safe sex" approach) and another that contained both abstinence and contraception content (i.e., comprehensive sex education), and found that neither program delayed or reduced teen sexual activity. Furthermore, these programs, whose main emphasis is on contraception, failed to increase use among adolescents.

Christine Kim and Robert Rector,
"Evidence on the Effectiveness of Abstinence Education:
An Update," The Heritage Foundation, February 19, 2010.

A study by University of Pennsylvania researchers released Feb. 2 [2010] found abstinence education is effective in delaying the onset of teen sexual activity. After eight hours of instruction on abstinence, middle school students were one third less likely to engage in sexual activity compared to their peers. This effect persisted two years after they attended the class.

By contrast, the study found both "safe sex" and "comprehensive sex-ed" programs ineffective. The former promote only use of contraceptives; the latter teach abstinence and contraception.

Published in the American Medical Association's *Archives of Pediatrics & Adolescent Medicine*, the Penn study used a randomized controlled experiment. The approach, designed to produce unbiased results, is considered the gold standard in program evaluation.

This is the most sophisticated evaluation showing abstinence education's positive results, but it's not the first. A 2008 research paper from The Heritage Foundation catalogued 15 scientific studies of abstinence education, 11 of which found positive effects.

Funding Abstinence Programs

On the same day the Penn researchers' study came out, President [Barack] Obama released his 2011 budget proposal. It zeroes out funding for abstinence education while creating a $179 million comprehensive sex-ed program—the very kind the Penn study shows to be ineffective. Add that to more than $600 million a year already spent by the Department of Health and Human Services on pregnancy and STD prevention programs and "family planning" services for teens.

The Obama administration's plans not only fly in the face of the research, they ignore the real needs of young women. Teen girls say they want to hear the abstinence message. More and more young women who have braved the casual-sex culture say they still haven't found what they're looking for.

If we want to empower these women, let's teach abstinence.

| "Abstinence-only education has become
emblematic of the rule of ideology over
science."

Abstinence for Teens Does Not Work

Ellen Goodman

Ellen Goodman is a columnist for the Boston Globe. *In the following viewpoint, she reviews some recent evidence that abstinence-only education does not work and reports that the only thing teens take away from abstinence education is a negative and inaccurate view of contraception. Goodman asserts that the federal government needs to stop funding these failed programs because abstinence for teens has been proven to be ineffective. The fact that the government increased funding for these programs during the administration of George W. Bush, Goodman contends, confirms the triumph of ideology over science and common sense.*

As you read, consider the following questions:

1. According to Goodman, how much was spent on abstinence education programs in 2008?

2. How many teens in ten does the author report have sex before they leave high school?

3. According to the author, what do the majority of protective parents want the outcomes of sex education programs to be for their teens?

I hate to bring this up right now when the ink is barely dry on your New Year's resolution. But if history is any guide, you are likely to fall off the assorted wagons to which you are currently lashed.

I don't say this to disparage your willpower. Hang onto that celery stick for dear life. And even if you stop doing those stomach crunches and start sneaking out for a smoke, at least you can comfort yourself with fond memories of your moment of resolution.

Taking the Pledge

Compare that to the factoid in the newest research about teens who pledge abstinence. The majority not only break the pledge, they forget they ever made it.

This study of about 1,000 teens comes from Johns Hopkins researcher Janet Rosenbaum, who compared teens who took a pledge of abstinence with teens of similar backgrounds and beliefs who didn't. She found absolutely no difference in their sexual behavior, or the age at which they began having sex, or the number of their partners.

In fact, the only difference was that the group that promised to remain abstinent was significantly less likely to use birth control, especially condoms, when they did have sex. The lesson many students seemed to retain from their abstinence-only program was a negative and inaccurate view of contraception.

This is not just a primer on the capacity for teenage denial or the inner workings of adolescent neurobiology. What makes this study important is this: "virginity pledges" are one of the

"AND IN THE MAGICAL KINGDOM OF 'HAPPY' NO ONE DID 'IT' UNTIL THE WEDDING. THE END."

ways that the government measures whether abstinence-only education is "working." They count the pledges as proof that teens will abstain. It turns out that this is like counting New Year's resolutions as proof that you lost 10 pounds.

We have been here before. And before that. And before that.

A Failed Policy

When he was running for president, [George W.] Bush promised, "My administration will elevate abstinence education from an afterthought to an urgent goal." Over the last eight years, a cottage industry of "abstinence-only until marriage" purveyors became a McMansion industry. Funding increased from $73 million a year in 2001 to $204 million in 2008. That's a total of $1.5 billion in federal money for an ideology in search of a methodology. And half the states refused funds to pay for sex mis-education.

By now, there's an archive of research showing that the binge was a bust. Programs mandated to teach only "the social, psychological and health gains (of) abstaining from sexual activity" and to warn of the dangers of having sex have been awarded failing grades for truth and effectiveness. As Rosenbaum says, "Abstinence-only education is required to give inaccurate information. Teens are savvy consumers of information and know what they are getting."

Our investment in abstinence-only may not be a scam on the scale of Bernie Madoff. But this industry has had standards for truth as loose as some mortgage lenders. All in all, abstinence-only education has become emblematic of the rule of ideology over science.

Sex Ed and Culture Wars

The sorry part is that sex education got caught in the culture wars. It's been framed, says Bill Albert of the National Campaign to Prevent Teen and Unplanned Pregnancy, as a battle between "those who wanted virginity pledges and those who wanted to hand out condoms to 14-year-olds."

Meanwhile, six in 10 teens have sex before they leave high school and 730,000 teenage girls will get pregnant this year. We see them everywhere from *Juno* to Juneau—or to be more accurate, Anchorage, where Sarah Palin, advocate of abstinence-only education, just became an unplanned grandparent.

What the overwhelming majority of protective parents actually want is not a political battle. They want teens to delay sex and to have honest information about sexuality, including contraception. The programs that work best combine those lessons.

Stop Funding Failure

Soon Congress and the new administration will be anteing up annual funding for abstinence-only programs. As Cecile Richards of Planned Parenthood says, abstinence-only education

183

was "an experiment gone awry. We spent $1.5 billion and can't point to a single study that says this helps. If it doesn't help, why fund it?"

Teens are not the only masters of denial. But we are finally stepping back from the culture wars. We are, with luck, returning to something that used to be redundant—evidence-based science. That's a pledge worth signing . . . and remembering.

> "Making the morning-after pill more readily available will also lower the number of abortions in this country and the number of children born to unprepared girls—many of whom are single and poor."

Teens Should Have Access to Emergency Contraception Without Parental Consent

Maura Kelly

Maura Kelly is a writer. In the following viewpoint, she applauds a recent legal decision to allow seventeen-year-old girls to obtain emergency contraception without a prescription from a doctor. Kelly notes that conservative opposition to the new rule is based on the mistaken belief that emergency contraception is tantamount to abortion—which it is not. She argues that women's groups should press for even more access, including making emergency contraception available over the counter to all females, regardless of age.

As you read, consider the following questions:

1. According to Kelly, who resigned over the US Food and Drug Administration's handling of access to emergency contraception?

2. How long did it take the George W. Bush administration to respond to a petition by women's groups to expand access to emergency contraception, according to Kelly?

3. According to the Guttmacher Institute, what percentage of females who have sex before the age of fourteen do so involuntarily?

Thanks to a ruling last week [March 22–28, 2009] by a wise federal judge, 17-year-old girls will now be able to obtain the morning-after pill without a prescription. (Previously, only those 18 and older could get the drug, known as Plan B, over the counter.) The [George W.] Bush administration held off on issuing a decision about making emergency contraception available to younger females, despite its efficacy and safety, because conservatives believe it's tantamount to abortion.

The Reality of Emergency Contraception

Oh, come on. The morning-after pill—which, despite its nickname, consists of two tablets—is essentially a megadose of the synthetic progestogen in the birth control pill. Opposing it is akin to saying girls shouldn't be using chemical contraception at all.

In his decision, US District Judge Edward Korman excoriated Bush's former lackeys at the US Food and Drug Administration (FDA), saying officials there had "repeatedly and unreasonably" delayed their decision for political reasons, rather than because of health concerns. "Indeed," he said, "the record is clear that the FDA's course of conduct regarding Plan B departed in significant ways from the agency's normal procedures regarding similar applications to switch a drug product from prescription to nonprescription use."

Susan Wood, former director of FDA's office of women's health, would agree with that. She resigned in 2005 as an expression of her dismay over the organisation's handling of the issue. Now a professor at George Washington University's school of public health, she applauded Korman's ruling, telling the Associated Press: "What happened with Plan B demonstrated that the agency was off track, and was not being allowed to do its job properly. This [ruling] is telling the FDA to move forward with a focus on good science."

Aiming for More Access

It certainly is. But that doesn't mean women's rights activists should let the FDA off the hook now. It's time to keep the pressure on to loosen the strictures even more. The petition introduced by the Association of Reproductive Health Professionals and 65 other groups in February 2001, calling for the FDA to make Plan B available over the counter to all females, regardless of age, should be reintroduced. (Bush's FDA took five years to respond, finally denying the petition in 2006.)

If the morning-after pill were available to more girls, it would not suddenly make them more likely to have intercourse or to practice unsafe sex, as conservative groups seem to think. (Incidentally, I beg those who think that preaching abstinence to teens is any kind of real solution to recall Bristol Palin's story, among others.)

It's not as if adolescent females are going to say to themselves, "Oh, I'll just use Plan B as my only form of birth control". Not when it costs $40 a pop (a significant amount for the average high schooler) and not when many teens are likely to feel ashamed or at least uncomfortable about buying it.

Preventing Unwanted Pregnancies

But making it easier to obtain will help prevent unwanted pregnancies for girls who were having sex when the condom

What Is Emergency Contraception?

Emergency contraception is a method of preventing pregnancy to be used after a contraceptive fails or after unprotected sex. It is not for routine use. Drugs used for this purpose are called emergency contraceptive pills, postcoital pills, or morning-after pills. Emergency contraceptives contain the hormones estrogen and progestin (levonorgestrel), either separately or in combination. FDA [US Food and Drug Administration] has approved two products for prescription use for emergency contraception—Preven (approved in 1998) and Plan B (approved in 1999).

What is Plan B?

Plan B is emergency contraception, a backup method to birth control. It is in the form of two levonorgestrel pills (0.75 mg in each pill) that are taken by mouth after unprotected sex. Levonorgestrel is a synthetic hormone used in birth control pills for over 35 years. Plan B can reduce a woman's risk of pregnancy when taken as directed if she has had unprotected sex. . . .

How does Plan B work?

Plan B works like other birth control pills to prevent pregnancy. Plan B acts primarily by stopping the release of an egg from the ovary (ovulation). It may prevent the union of sperm and egg (fertilization). If fertilization does occur, Plan B may prevent a fertilized egg from attaching to the womb (implantation). If a fertilized egg is implanted prior to taking Plan B, Plan B will not work.

"FDA's Decision Regarding Plan B: Questions and Answers," US Food and Drug Administration, 2011. www.fda.gov.

slipped or broke; for girls who forgot to take their contraception; and, particularly, for girls who were coerced into having unprotected sex, or were raped. (Seventy-four percent of females who have sex before the age of 14 do so involuntarily, according to the Guttmacher Institute.)

Making the morning-after pill more readily available will also lower the number of abortions in this country and the number of children born to unprepared girls—many of whom are single and poor. Young mothers frequently don't have the resources, financially or emotionally, to be good parents.

That's especially true when the pregnancies are unplanned. When they can't handle the burden, society must help them shoulder it. Let's make their lives—and ours—easier by making Plan B available to anyone who needs it.

| "It is important that people understand what 'emergency contraception' drugs ... actually do. The bottom line is that while they sometimes prevent pregnancy, other times they terminate it, killing the new human life."

Teens Should Not Have Access to Emergency Contraception Without Parental Consent

F.K. Bartels

F.K. Bartels is a writer and contributor to the Catholic Online website. In the following viewpoint, he criticizes a recent legal decision that makes emergency contraception accessible to seventeen-year-old girls without a prescription. Bartels contends that emergency contraception can inhibit implantation of a fertilized egg that is tantamount to an abortion. He points out that this is against Catholic Church doctrine and that young women who take emergency contraception without consulting a doctor or their parents may experience serious psychological anguish later in life because of their actions. Bartels laments what he characterizes as a culture of death that allows abortion to be undertaken too easily.

As you read, consider the following questions:

1. According to the author, in how many countries is levonorgestrel, the most common kind of emergency contraception, available?

2. What does the Catechism of the Catholic Church say is intrinsically evil, according to the author?

3. When does the Catholic Church teach that life begins, according to Bartels?

Yet another chemical weapon has reared its ugly head, directed at the once safest place on earth, a mother's womb. The London Associated Press [AP] reported that a "new type of morning-after pill" has been developed which is "more effective than the most widely used drug." It is allegedly taken to prevent pregnancies, according to a report published in the *British Medical Journal.*

The Introduction of ellaOne

The new drug, *ulipristal acetate*, sold as *ellaOne* [sold as ella in the United States], is currently available in Europe with a doctor's prescription and is reported to "work" for up to 5 days after having "unprotected" sex. While the drug is not legally available elsewhere, given FDA [U.S. Food and Drug Administration] trends it is likely the drug will become available for purchase in the U.S. once the required studies have been completed.

The AP reported that "levonorgestrel, the most widely used emergency contraceptive pill, is only effective if women take it within three days of having sex. It is sold under various brand names including Levonelle and Plan B and is available in more than 140 countries, including the United States, Canada and many countries in Western Europe. In nearly 50 of those countries women can get it without a prescription."

In 2006, the U.S. became one of the countries in which women can obtain Plan B without a prescription, provided they were eighteen years of age or older. However, on March 23, 2009, U.S. District Judge Edward Korman of New York ordered the Food and Drug Administration to allow 17-year-old girls to purchase Plan B over the counter. Judge Korman also directed the FDA to reevaluate lifting all age restrictions.

What Does Emergency Contraception Do?

It is important that people understand what "emergency contraception" drugs like ulipristal acetate and levonorgestrel (Plan B pill) actually do. The bottom line is that while they sometimes prevent pregnancy, other times they terminate it, killing the new human life. They often act as abortifacients.

The FDA reports that "Plan B . . . is believed to act as an emergency contraceptive principally by preventing ovulation or fertilization (by altering tubal transport of sperm and/or ova). In addition, it may inhibit implantation (by altering the endometrium). It is not effective once the process of implantation has begun."

Note the FDA states that Plan B "may inhibit implantation." A fertilized egg that is prevented from implantation dies as a result. This is killing plain and simple. It is an attack on innocent human life; it is one person saying to another, "I am sovereign ruler over your life. I hereby deny your right to life." Further, whether or not emergency contraceptive drugs "principally" act by preventing ovulation or fertilization does not mean that their use is not immoral.

A Morally Deplorable Act

The Catechism of the Catholic Church reminds us that contraceptive use is intrinsically evil: ". . . every action which, whether in anticipation of the conjugal act, or its accomplish-

Is Plan B an Abortifacient Drug or a Contraceptive?

Numerous studies support the notion that the high dose, high powered steroid(s) found in emergency abortion drugs like Plan B are abortifacient 75 to 89% of the time. Rarely will a drug like Plan B work to suppress ovulation and truly prevent the meeting of the male and female gametes PRIOR to the moment of conception.

"Plan B [Emergency Abortion Pill] FAQs," Pharmacists for Life International, 2011. www.pfli.org.

ment, or in the development of its natural consequences, proposes, whether as an end or as a means, to render procreation impossible" is intrinsically evil.

The manner in which these "new drugs" are being trumpeted as "more effective at preventing unwanted pregnancies" is deplorable. Since when are people "unwanted" items which may be disposed of at will? Since when may a child be extinguished at whim by purchasing an innocuous looking, neatly wrapped package and popping a few pills? As dark as these inclinations are many have arrived at them—in fact embraced them—due to the worship of unmoored and uninhibited sexual "pleasure."

Drug companies rush to meet these "needs" of modern man, whether they be immoral matters little, for the bottom line is profit. In their laboratories they employ "mad scientists" who labor away day by day, concocting the next weapon which will be wielded against human life, a weapon which will advance the culture of death and the worship of this false god. Those deluded by the lie fork out millions upon millions of dollars in order to satiate this desire for unrestrained sex with no consequences.

The American Culture of Death

This mind-set is a by-product of the culture of death. It manifests itself in comments like this one found on the FDA website: "Any families with teen girls should have access over the counter to Plan B, as should any women of childbearing age. . . . Plan B helps the women [sic] flush the horror away of conquest, humiliation, and loss of control." Such comments shine a spotlight on the present darkness.

Where do we even begin in countering these malevolent attitudes? "Any families with teen girls should have access over the counter" to chemical weapons which often kill children? And if a woman experiences the "horror" of "conquest, humiliation, and loss of control," she ought to, therefore, pop a pill and possibly kill her unborn child? The type of thinking displayed in the comment is so far from reasonable, so dark, so impoverished that it is difficult to understand how a person could have actually written it, let alone believed it. This type of thinking is capable of inflicting severe damage not only on the child in the sanctuary of the womb but the woman ingesting the chemical weapon.

While some women are not immediately aware of the deadly nature of these chemical weapons, a woman who has consumed them is likely to one day realize she might possibly have killed her unborn child: intense emotional and spiritual suffering flows from such a realization. These chemical weapons can turn women into postabortion mothers whose lives are lived in a private hell as a result of the nearly unbearable guilt and sadness experienced through coming face to face with the reality of abortion.

It Should Not Be So Easy to End a Life

We can only speculate as to how many unborn children die each day as a result of these deadly weapons marketed as nice little tablets which are the "answer" to the "problem" of "unwanted pregnancies." And that is part of the dilemma, isn't it?

Our culture is programmed to look for an answer to every ailment in a pill. Depressed? No problem. There's a pill for that. Can't sleep? There's a pill for that too. Anxious? Relief is as close as the drugstore.

"Unprotected" sex? Not to worry. Just pop a little, cheap, easy-to-swallow pill. While there may be a false intellectual disconnect from the abortive capabilities of these chemical weapons, the truth is that in swallowing one of these deadly pills people become accomplices in the very darkest inclinations of the culture of death.

It has been the constant teaching of the Catholic Church that human life begins at the moment of conception. We all had a beginning and that moment we became a person. If we are a person now, we were a person that first moment we began to exist, that moment in which our father's sperm joined with our mother's egg. It is at that moment, at conception, that human life begins and a human person exists. Science has confirmed this fact again and again. The Natural Law written on every human heart has revealed it to our conscience. If a chemical weapon had poisoned any one of us at that moment, we would not be here. We all know that would be unjust.

The Catholic Church's Statement on the Morning-After Pill

The Pontifical Academy for Life released a statement on October 31, 2000, explaining the real dangers of "morning-after" pills: "The morning-after pill is a hormone-based preparation . . . which, within and no later than 72 hours after a presumably fertile act of sexual intercourse, has a predominantly 'anti-implantation' function, i.e., it prevents a possible fertilized ovum (which is a human embryo), by now in the *blastocyst* stage of its development (fifth to sixth day after fertilization), from being implanted in the uterine wall by a process of altering the wall itself. The final result will thus be the expulsion and loss of this embryo." Note that Plan B has that same "anti-implantation" function as the FDA website attests. We have no reason to believe that anti-life drugs like ulipristal acetate will not operate to some extent in the same manner.

The bottom line is that these chemical weapons can be destroyers of children. They are also deadly in many other ways. Unfortunately, our secularist society is intent on promoting their use ever more widely, making them available over the counter to as many women as possible. This is nothing more than people encouraging people to kill other people. It is insanity.

As Catholics, we are called to humanize the societies and nations in which we live; to encourage others to live under the full light and love of God's plan of salvation as fully human persons in solidarity. We want the world to be a better place. It does not get better by making it easier to kill innocent children with chemical weapons directed at the sanctuary of the womb.

> "Making condoms available to students doesn't make them more likely to have intercourse. It just makes the intercourse that students are having that much safer."

Condoms Should Be Available in Schools

Kate Dailey

Kate Dailey is a senior articles editor at Newsweek. *In the following viewpoint, she asserts that having condoms available in schools does not make students more likely to have sex—it just means that the sex they are having is safe sex. Dailey argues that it is unrealistic to think that preteens and teenagers are not having sex, and having a trained counselor and condoms available is only being practical. In particular, she maintains that such a program is a benefit for young people who are not able to talk to their parents honestly about their sex lives.*

As you read, consider the following questions:

1. In a study of Philadelphia schools, how much did the rate of sexual activity drop with students that had condoms available in schools?

2. What factors does the author say will make students want to have sex?

3. According to a study by the Centers for Disease Control and Prevention, what percentage of girls and boys aged eighteen to nineteen have talked to their parents about sex?

"Condoms for kindergartners" is a very catchy slogan, but as an explanation of the much-maligned Province-town, Mass., school-board policy to help prevent both STDs [sexually transmitted diseases] and unwanted pregnancy, it pretty much misses the mark.

The policy, left intentionally open-ended, allows any student who is considering sexual activity to request condoms from the school nurse. That student would first get counseling—including abstinence education. The parents would not be informed.

So theoretically, yes, a 6-year-old could walk in and request condoms. The chances of that happening, of course, are slim—but if a 6-year-old were asking about sex, wouldn't a little counseling from a medical professional be in order?

Studies Show No Link Between Access to Condoms and Increased Sexual Activity

So let's disabuse the notion put forth by Kris Mineau, president of the Massachusetts Family Institute, who was quoted in the *Boston Globe* as saying, "This is the theater of the absurd to hand condoms to first graders who don't even know what their purpose possibly could be, who can't even spell sex," he said. First graders who can't spell "sex" won't go seeking out condoms. And putting condoms in the nurse's office won't suddenly make those kids start having S-E-X-ual thoughts.

Study after study show that making condoms available to students doesn't make them more likely to have intercourse. It just makes the intercourse that students are having that much safer. A few studies have shown *lower* rates of sexual activity in schools that offer free condoms: One study of Philadelphia schools showed rates of sexual activity drop from 64 to 58 percent in schools with condoms versus a 3 percent increase in schools without.

That is because condoms don't make kids have sex. Hormones make kids have sex. Peer pressure makes kids have sex. Super-sexualized television, movies, and music videos make kids have sex. The kids who want to have sex, who are coursing with hormones and are super-hot for one another and have brains that can't yet process long-term consequences nor provide much in the way of impulse control, are going to have sex with or without condoms.

However, not all kids who have sex feel this way. There are kids who want to have sex because they're getting pressure from their boyfriend or girlfriend, because they're trying to get over the guy from Glee Club who dumped them, or because they want to prove they're not a kid anymore. Those kids are the ones who would most benefit from this program: kids who go to the nurse to get condoms and end up getting advice and reassurance that they don't have to have sex on someone else's time line.

Preteens Need Access to Condoms

OK, fine—so why not make this very adult counseling/condom distribution available only to teenagers? Those are the kids with hormones; those are the kids who feel the most pressure to fit in. Why bother innocent middle school kids—or worse, kids in the fifth grade and younger—about such complicated issues?

As nice as it would be to think that all 11-year-olds, or 10-year-olds, or 13-year-olds, are immune from sexual pressure, that's not the case: Kids develop on different time lines, and kids date outside their age range. A study in the *Journal of*

Teens and Condoms

From 1995 through 2006–2010, the data show that virtually all sexually experienced teenagers have used some method of contraception. Since 1995, more than 96% of sexually experienced female teenagers had ever used a contraceptive method. The most commonly used method among teenagers in 2006–2010 remained the condom (reported by 96% of females), followed by withdrawal (57%) and the pill (56%). Since 2002, the use of highly effective hormonal contraceptive injectables (primarily Depo-Provera) remained stable. About 20% of females in 2002 and 2006–2010 reported using hormonal contraceptive injectables.

Use of the contraceptive patch by teenagers increased significantly from about 2% in 2002, when it was newly introduced, to 10% by 2006–2010. Since 2002, the use of emergency contraception has significantly increased, from 8% in 2002 to 14% in 2006–2010. The percentage of sexually experienced teenaged females ever using periodic abstinence, or the calendar rhythm method, appeared to increase from 11% in 2002 to 15% in 2006–2010, but this observed difference was not statistically significant. A small percentage of teenagers (5.2%) had used the recently introduced contraceptive ring.

"Teenagers in the United States:
Sexual Activity, Contraceptive Use, and Childbearing,
2006–2010 National Survey of Family Growth,"
Centers for Disease Control and Prevention,
October 2011. www.cdc.gov.

Adolescent Health found that more than 40 percent of middle school students interviewed at one school dated someone two years older or more, and of those students (median age: 11

and a half), they were 30 times more likely to have had sex. And those are the kids most in need of the counseling provided by a caring adult.

Condom Access Policy Should Be Based on Facts, Not Fantasies

To argue that the caring adult in question should be a parent is admirable, but it's as unrealistic as saying that 12-year-olds just don't have sex. If parents want their kids to come to them when they're ready for sex, then it's up to the parents to establish an open and comfortable relationship. And if you, as a parent, have built that relationship with your kid, congratulations! But not everyone has such a stellar support system. A CDC [Centers for Disease Control and Prevention] study shows that only 48.5 percent of girls and 35 percent of boys ages 18 and 19 had talked to their parents about safe sex.

So having a school nurse trained on how to talk to kids about safe sex, available to talk to kids about sex, and providing access to reliable birth control is a really good thing for kids: It helps kids who are going to have sex anyway do it safely. It helps kids who are unsure to sort out their feelings. And it provides the education that doesn't always come from home, even if some people think it should.

Now the school district is considering rewriting the policy so that the counseling is available only to students in the fifth grade and up. In practice, it probably won't make much of a difference, and the district was right to value the safety of its students over the moral hand-wringing of well-meaning but uninformed parents and pundits. But it's a shame it had to face such scorn and derision in the first place. The kids in Provincetown are safer now than they were last year—but how many other schools decided that enacting a similar policy just wasn't worth the bad PR?

> *"Instead of giving us condoms, schools should give us knowledge about how we can effectively abstain."*

Condoms Should Not Be Available in Schools

Kanisha King

Kanisha King is a staff writer for Vox: The Voice of Our Generation. *In the following viewpoint, she contends that teens are not mature enough to use condoms consistently or correctly. King argues that abstinence should be the only message for teens, because it is the only surefire protection against sexually transmitted diseases and unplanned pregnancy. Schools need to promote self-control and provide moral role models to encourage teens to practice abstinence, she argues, which is why she believes that condoms in schools are a mistake.*

As you read, consider the following questions:

1. According to a 2006 study, were teens more likely to use condoms with partners they considered serious or those they considered casual partners?

2. According to the American Social Health Association, what percentage of all new HIV infections occur in teens?

3. According to the author, what should teens be focusing on instead of sex?

I've seen enough of my close friends and family members get pregnant as teenagers to know that sex—without protection—is what's on the minds of many teens today. Sure, most teens know they should use a condom to reduce their risk of pregnancy and sexually transmitted infections (STIs), but most teens are inconsistent, according to a 2006 study of 1,300 adolescents ages 15 to 21 in Atlanta, Miami and Providence, R.I., conducted by researchers at the Bradley Hasbro Children's Research Center and Brown [Alpert] Medical School in Rhode Island.

The study found teens were more likely to not use condoms with partners whom they considered serious as opposed to casual partners. More than 19 million new cases of STIs occur every year—and nearly 50 percent involve people between 15 and 24. Half of all new HIV infections occur in teenagers, according to the American Social Health Association.

Practicing abstinence is the most effective way to prevent pregnancy. Abstinence can help us live disease-free, successful lives by helping us focus on our educational and life goals because we're not preoccupied with having sex. That's why I believe that distributing condoms to teens at Georgia schools would be a mistake.

Can Doesn't Mean Should

It is clear that we teens have not proven ourselves to be responsible enough to have sex. Parents, teachers and adults tell us to use condoms. But teens ignore their advice.

Many of us cannot even remember to turn in a homework assignment when it is due, so I don't know why people would think we're responsible enough to use condoms effectively every single time we have sex.

For me, it's easier to say no than it is to remember to have and use a condom. I know what I want out of life, and that doesn't involve having a baby while I'm a teenager. I saw how hard it was for my friends and family members who got pregnant as teens to accomplish their goals when they had their kids. I know that I don't want to risk my future—even with a condom.

Are Teens Responsible Enough?

Some people feel that distributing condoms in school is the key to solving the STI epidemic and lowering the teen pregnancy rate. But I don't think that teens are emotionally mature and responsible enough. Handing out condoms in schools won't solve teens' problems. Teens should focus on their education and career goals; giving them condoms will help them focus on sex instead of their education. Giving out condoms will only make us more curious and expose us to situations we have no business being in, such as getting STDs [sexually transmitted diseases] or having a child—problems that we can avoid totally by saying no to sex.

When schools distribute condoms, they tell students to protect themselves from STIs and pregnancy. But what if that condom fails or rips, or there's a hole in it? Who is going to be blamed—the condom company, the student or the school? The back of the condom box says condoms "will help reduce the risk." It does not say that it will protect you 100% of the time or that it eliminates the risk of pregnancy, sexually transmitted infections and emotional consequences of teenage sex.

I often hear adults say, "Take care of yourself." Just because we can use a condom doesn't mean that we can take care of ourselves. Abstinence shows that we can take responsibility, and saying we want to wait shows a lot about our character. Instead of giving teens condoms, more adults need to emphasize that teens should practice self-control.

Why Abstinence Is a Smart Choice

If we had more positive role models to teach us about abstinence and give us real advice about how to wait, rather than giving us condoms and promoting sex, more of us might start to practice abstinence. Instead of giving us condoms, schools should give us knowledge about how we can effectively abstain.

Periodical and Internet Sources Bibliography

The following articles have been selected to supplement the diverse views presented in this chapter.

Jill U. Adams	"Teens and the Morning After Pill," *Los Angeles Times*, April 6, 2009.
Heather Corinna	"Get Real! Should I Feel Bad About Taking Plan B?," RH Reality Check, July 18, 2008. www.rhrealitycheck.org.
M. Jocelyn Elders	"A Collision of Culture and Nature: How Our Fear of Teen Sexuality Leaves Teens More Vulnerable," RH Reality Check, July 19, 2011. www.rhrealitycheck.org.
Mike Galanos	"Plan B Risky for 17-Year-Old Girls," CNN.com, April 30, 2009.
Elisabeth Garber-Paul	"A New Plan for Plan B," RH Reality Check, April 8, 2009. www.rhrealitycheck.org.
Elizabeth Hovde	"Sex Ed for Teens: Today's Abstinence Programs Are Worth Their Funding," *Oregonian*, October 10, 2009.
Roland Martin	"Sex Education Should Be Mandatory in All Schools," CNN.com, October 29, 2011.
Mike McManus	"Plan B Is a Terrible Plan for Teens," VirtueOnline.org, March 27, 2009.
Jack Nicas	"Condoms Old News in Many Schools," *Boston Globe*, June 28, 2010.
Amy Sullivan	"How to Bring an End to the War over Sex Ed," *Time*, March 19, 2009.

For Further Discussion

Chapter 1

1. Naomi Cahn and June Carbone contend that birth control has benefited society and is conducive to feminist values. In his viewpoint, Timothy Reichert argues that birth control has been damaging to society and hurts women. With which viewpoint do you agree, and why?

2. There is a persistent debate as to whether birth control increases or decreases the number of abortions in the United States. Read viewpoints written by Thomas Peters and Frosty Wooldridge. Which author makes the more persuasive argument, and why?

3. What are the moral and ethical concerns over the new emergency contraceptive ella? After reading viewpoints by Sarah Richards and Michael Fragoso, offer your own opinion on the morality and ethics involved. Use information from the viewpoints to support your answer.

Chapter 2

1. Susan Jacoby believes that the birth control pill benefits women. Others argue that the birth control pill is destructive for women and society. What do you think the impact of the birth control pill has been? Has it been good for women? For society? Explain your reasoning.

2. Michael Parsons, Tracy Clark-Flory, and Greg Laden discuss the implications of a male birth control pill. What aspect of this new reproductive technology do you think is most beneficial? Which is the most problematic? Explain.

Chapter 3

1. Should there be religious exemptions for universal birth control coverage? Read viewpoints by Hannah C. Smith and Nancy Northup. Which author makes the best argument for her view, and why?

2. Joel Connelly believes that pharmacists have the right to refuse to dispense birth control. Jack Marshall argues that pharmacists should not have that right. After reading both viewpoints, what is your opinion on the issue?

Chapter 4

1. What kind of sex education is best for young people? Jennifer Marshall maintains that teaching only abstinence is the most appropriate and effective, while Ellen Goodman argues that abstinence education doesn't work. Read both viewpoints and present your opinion on the issue. What kind of sex education is offered by your school?

2. The ability of teens to get emergency contraception with parental consent has garnered controversy in recent years. Maura Kelly asserts that there are sound reasons for allowing such a policy. F.K. Bartels argues that it is unsound public policy. Which author makes a more compelling argument, and why?

Organizations to Contact

The editors have compiled the following list of organizations concerned with the issues debated in this book. The descriptions are derived from materials provided by the organizations. All have publications or information available for interested readers. The list was compiled on the date of publication of the present volume; the information provided here may change. Be aware that many organizations take several weeks or longer to respond to inquiries, so allow as much time as possible.

Advocates for Youth
2000 M Street NW, Suite 750, Washington, DC   20036
(202) 419-3420 • fax: (202) 419-1448
website: www.advocatesforyouth.org

Advocates for Youth is an organization that works in the United States and developing countries to create responsible and effective sexual health strategies for adolescents and to disseminate accurate information about contraception, sexually transmitted diseases (STDs), and reproductive health. Its ultimate goal is to provide young people with the tools they need to make responsible decisions about sexual behavior and family planning. One of the organization's key programs is the Adolescent Contraceptive Access Initiative, which focuses on offering accurate information on birth control options for young people. The Advocates for Youth website has a range of publications available, including reports, fact sheets, training materials for volunteers, and assessments of various programs around the world. It also publishes a blog, which features news and updates on current events sponsored by the organization, and provides podcasts from experts and staff who discuss programs and policy debates.

American Life League (ALL)

PO Box 1350, Stafford, VA   22555

(540) 659-4171 • fax: (540) 659-2586

website: www.all.org

The American Life League's "The Pill Kills" campaign seeks to warn the public of the dangers of the birth control pill. ALL outlines the many side effects of the pill, citing specific cases of women suffering permanent physical damage and even death as a result of birth control pill use. ALL also warns that the pill is harmful to marriages, because it limits procreation, interrupts bonding between spouses, and lowers a woman's libido. Its website offers links to talking points, related news items, and opportunities to participate in protest activities opposing the use and sale of oral contraceptives.

Association of Reproductive Health Professionals (ARHP)

1901 L Street NW, Suite 300, Washington, DC   20036

(202) 446-3825

e-mail: ARHP@arhp.org

website: www.arhp.org

The Association of Reproductive Health Professionals (ARHP) is a medical association composed of reproductive health professionals interested in networking and disseminating the most effective and up-to-date information on programs, policies, technology, and medical breakthroughs. The ARHP develops evidence-based programs for its members whose goals are to provide the best care to their patients. The ARHP website offers interactive tools for patients searching for accurate information on contraception, sexually transmitted diseases (STDs), and other issues of reproductive health. The official journal of ARHP, *Contraception: An International Reproductive Health Journal*, features groundbreaking research and commentary on hot topics in reproductive health.

Bixby Center for Global Reproductive Health

3333 California Street, Suite 335, Box 0744
San Francisco, CA   94143
(415) 502-4086 • fax: (415) 502-8479
e-mail: loewl@obgyn.ucfs.edu
website: bixbycenter.ucsf.edu

The Bixby Center for Global Reproductive Health was established in 1999 by the University of California, San Francisco to develop strategies to address domestic and international health problems. The Bixby Center outlines its goals as formulating new reproductive health technologies in contraception and reproductive and maternal health; decreasing maternal mortality; training practitioners and researchers; conducting policy analyses and research in the field; and improving adolescent reproductive health. The Bixby Center website offers access to a range of reports on contraception and reproductive health, fact sheets, monographs and books, videos, and issue briefs.

Center for Reproductive Rights

120 Wall Street, New York, NY   10005
(917) 637-3600 • fax: (917) 637-3666
e-mail: info@reprorights.org
website: reproductiverights.org

The Center for Reproductive Rights is a global legal center that works to secure women's reproductive rights and access to contraception and family planning services. To this end, it has presented and defended cases before national courts, United Nations committees, and regional human rights bodies. The center also works with policy makers and legislators to strengthen sound and effective reproductive laws in the United States and around the world. The group's website features access to a range of in-depth reports, press releases, surveys, fact sheets, policy briefs, and information on reproductive law and policy. Also available is *ReproWrites*, the center's monthly e-newsletter, which provides updates on recent initiatives and current news.

Institute of Medicine (IOM)

2100 C Street NW, Washington, DC   20037
(202) 334-2352
e-mail: iomwww@nas.edu
website: www.iom.edu

The Institute of Medicine (IOM) was established in 1970 as the health division of the National Academy of Sciences. The IOM is an independent and nonpartisan organization that "serves as the advisor to the nation to improve health." It does this by conducting extensive research on the nation's emerging health problems and then consulting with and advising policy makers and legislators on developing sound public health policy. One of its primary responsibilities is organizing forums, roundtables, conferences, seminars, and other activities that work to facilitate debate, conversation, and the exchange of information. The IOM website offers access to hundreds of in-depth reports and studies published by the organization as well as videos of lectures, speeches, and expert panels.

International Consortium for Emergency Contraception (ICEC)

558 Broadway, Suite 503, New York, NY   10012
(212) 941-5300
e-mail: info@cecinfo.org
website: www.cecinfo.org

The International Consortium for Emergency Contraception (ICEC) is an association of seven international family planning organizations working to ensure that women have access to safe and effective emergency contraception. ICEC's advocacy efforts are focused in four main areas: emergency contraception and youth; legal challenges; improving and ensuring access; and providing services to women in crisis situations. ICEC publishes a biannual newsletter that features updates on the advocacy and legal efforts, announces upcoming events, and covers relevant issues.

National Family Planning & Reproductive Health Association (NFPRHA)

1627 K Street NW, 12th Floor, Washington, DC   20006
(202) 293-3114
e-mail: info@nfprha.org
website: www.nfprha.org

The National Family Planning & Reproductive Health Association (NFPRHA) is a member organization that advocates for health care administrators and professionals who serve low-income patients in the family planning and reproductive health field. It also works to provide training and continuing education for its members. NFPRHA is committed to providing high-quality, federally funded family planning care. The organization's website offers access to press releases, videos, and family planning profiles, which chronicle the work NFPRHA does to help patients across the country.

Pharmacists for Life International (PFLI)

PO Box 1281, Powell, OH   43065
(740) 881-5520 • fax: (740) 206-1260
e-mail: pfli@pfli.org
website: www.pfli.org

Pharmacists for Life International is a nonprofit organization made up of pharmacists and other pharmacy personnel who oppose the use of birth control or emergency contraception and support pharmacists' right to refuse to dispense such medications. The organization promotes education for pharmacists and medical personnel as well as for the general public on the threats to the sanctity of life presented by birth control. Its website provides numerous links to news items and scientific publications as well as to papers, fact sheets, and blogs authored by leaders of PFLI and affiliated organizations.

Planned Parenthood Federation of America (PPFA)

1110 Vermont Avenue NW, Suite 300, Washington, DC   20005
(202) 973-4800 • fax: (202) 296-3242
website: www.plannedparenthood.org

Planned Parenthood Federation of America (PPFA) is a non-profit organization that provides reproductive health and family planning services. The US affiliate of the International Planned Parenthood Federation (IPPF), the PPFA can be traced back to 1916, when family planning pioneer Margaret Sanger opened the country's first birth control clinic in Brooklyn, New York. Today, PPFA operates more than eight hundred health centers across the country that focus on high-quality and affordable health care. Another mission of PPFA is to educate American youth accurately and honestly about birth control choices and provide access to legal contraception. The organization publishes a number of fact sheets, studies, and news reports that can be found on the PPFA website.

Reproductive Health Access Project (RHAP)
PO Box 21191, New York, NY   10025
(917) 586-3260 • fax: (314) 584-3260
e-mail: info@reproductiveaccess.org
website: www.reproductiveaccess.org

The Reproductive Health Access Project (RHAP) is an organization that works "to ensure that women and teens at every socioeconomic level can readily obtain birth control and abortion from their own primary care clinician." To accomplish this goal, RHAP provides training, advocacy, and mentoring programs to support family physicians and local reproductive health services. RHAP publishes a biannual newsletter that is available on the organization's website.

US Department of Health and Human Services (HHS)
200 Independence Avenue SW, Washington, DC   20201
(877) 696-6775
website: www.hhs.gov

The US Department of Health and Human Services (HHS) is the government agency in charge of protecting the health of and providing essential health services to all Americans. HHS works closely with state and local governments to develop programs and implement policies. It is the goal of the HHS to

have a variety of safe and effective birth control options for American women and provide accurate and up-to-date information on such products. The HHS website offers a series of fact sheets on different birth control options as well as other educational information.

US Food and Drug Administration (FDA)

10903 New Hampshire Avenue, Silver Spring, MD   20993
(888) 463-6332
website: www.fda.gov

The US Food and Drug Administration (FDA) is an agency of the US Department of Health and Human Services (HHS) tasked with protecting public health through the testing, regulation, and supervision of contraception, prescription and over-the-counter medications, food safety, biopharmaceuticals, medical devices, and more. The FDA is the agency in charge of testing and regulating emergency contraception, as well as determining how birth control will be available. Information on how such decisions are made, in addition to press releases and studies, can be found on the FDA's website.

Bibliography of Books

Jean H. Baker   *Margaret Sanger: A Life of Passion.* New York: Hill & Wang, 2011.

Barbara Bonnekessen   *Of Homunculus Born: A Short History of Invisible Women.* Lanham, MD: University Press of America, 2012.

Allan Carlson   *Godly Seed: American Evangelicals Confront Birth Control, 1873–1973.* New Brunswick, NJ: Transaction Publishers, 2012.

Sherry F. Colb   *When Sex Counts: Making Babies and Making Law.* Lanham, MD: Rowman & Littlefield, 2007.

Laura Eldridge   *In Our Control: The Complete Guide to Contraceptive Choices for Women.* New York: Seven Stories Press, 2010.

Jessica Fields   *Risky Lessons: Sex Education and Social Inequality.* New Brunswick, NJ: Rutgers University Press, 2008.

Angel M. Foster and Lisa L. Wynn, eds.   *Emergency Contraception: The Story of a Global Reproductive Health Technology.* New York: Palgrave Macmillan, 2012.

Susan K. Freeman   *Sex Goes to School: Girls and Sex Education Before the 1960s.* Urbana: University of Illinois Press, 2008.

Christine J. Gardner — *Making Chastity Sexy: The Rhetoric of Evangelical Abstinence Campaigns.* Berkeley: University of California Press, 2011.

Miriam Grossman — *You're Teaching My Child What?: A Physician Exposes the Lies of Sex Education and How They Harm Your Child.* Washington, DC: Regnery Publishing, 2009.

Melissa Haussman — *Reproductive Rights and the State: Getting the Birth-Control, RU-486, and Morning-After Pills and the Gardasil Vaccine to the U.S. Market.* Westport, CT: Praeger, 2012.

Rose Holz — *The Birth Control Clinic in a Marketplace World.* Rochester, NY: Rochester Press, 2012.

Alexandra M. Lord — *Condom Nation: The U.S. Government's Sex Education Campaign from World War I to the Internet.* Baltimore, MD: Johns Hopkins University Press, 2010.

Kristin Luker — *When Sex Goes to School: Warring Views on Sex—and Sex Education—Since the Sixties.* New York: W.W. Norton & Co., 2006.

Kekla Magoon — *Sex Education in Schools.* Edina, MN: ABDO, 2010.

Elaine Tyler May — *America and the Pill: A History of Promise, Peril, and Liberation.* New York: Basic Books, 2010.

Ian Milsom, ed.   *Contraception and Family Planning.*
                       New York: Elsevier, 2006.

Jamie L. Mullaney   *Everyone Is NOT Doing It: Abstinence
                       and Personal Identity.* Chicago:
                       University of Chicago Press, 2006.

Leonard J. Nelson   *Diagnosis Critical: The Urgent Threats
III   Confronting Catholic Health Care.*
                       Huntington, IN: Our Sunday Visitor,
                       2009.

Carl Olson, ed.   *Celibacy and Religious Traditions.*
                       New York: Oxford University Press,
                       2008.

Shawn Lawrence   *Fool Me Twice: Fighting the Assault on
Otto   Science in America.* New York:
                       Rodale, 2011.

Heather Munro   *The Morning After: A History of
Prescott   Emergency Contraception in the
                       United States.* New Brunswick, NJ:
                       Rutgers University Press, 2011.

Isabella E. Rossi,   *Abstinence Education.* New York:
ed.   Nova Science Publishers, 2009.

Rickie Solinger   *Reproductive Politics: What Everyone
                       Needs to Know.* New York: Oxford
                       University Press, 2012.

Index

A

Abortion
conscience clauses/refusal to perform, 134, 135
contraception decreases abortions, 47, 53, 56, 57, 67, 189
contraception increases abortions, 44, 47–52
costs, 44–45
deaths, illegal, 88
decreasing need, as goal, 23–24
ella (emergency contraception) causes, 73–80, 145, 191
emergency contraception does not cause, 63–67
emergency contraception equated, 66–67, 185, 186, 190–191, 192, 193–196
emergency contraception's similarities, and implications, 59–62, 69, 77, 134
emotional outcomes, 45, 190–191, 194
following failed contraception, 44, 51
legislation banning, 67, 128
rates, annual, 54
rates, historical, 44, 67
rates, increasing, 49–50, 56
re-defining, 67, 135
See also Abortion pills
Abortion pills, 21, 60, 61, 66, 69, 71, 74, 76, 78, 145, 193
ella as, 21, 73, 74, 76, 78–80, 145
Plan B as abortifacient, 193

pollution, 101–102
subsidized insurance coverage, 142, 145, 148
Abstinence
history of birth control, 15, 88
practical advice desired, 205
promotion, 172, 177, 183, 202–205
See also Abstinence-only sex education
Abstinence-only sex education, 25, 172–174, 175
does not work, 180–184
evidence supporting, 177–179
funding, 172, 174, 179, 180, 182, 183–184
See also Abstinence
Abzug, Bella, 130, 131
ACLU (American Civil Liberties Union), 172
Adolescent Family Life Act (1981), 172
Adolescents. *See* Minors
Adoption
programs promoting, 172
unwed mothers' experiences, 88
Afghanistan conflict, 2001-, 57, 58
African American families
out-of-wedlock births, 29
single-parent, 55
African American women, 43
Age issues, emergency contraception, 185, 186, 190, 192, 194
Age of first sexual activity
coercion, 189, 199

Virginity pledges, 181–182, 183
Vitellogenesis, 107–108

W

Walsh, Mary Ann, 155
War on Poverty (United States), 27–29, 30
"War on Women," 22–23, 24–25
Wars, costs, 57, 58
Washington, prescriptions issues, 136, 157, 158–161
Water resources
  birth control hormone pollution, 100, 101–102, 103, 107–108
  condom pollution, 110
  human drinking and use, 54
  industrial and agricultural pollution, 105, 107, 108, 109, 110–111, 112
Watson Pharmaceuticals, 71, 79–80
"Week-after pill." See ella (emergency contraception drug)
Welfare system, US
  abstinence-only programs, 172
  birth control access, 30
  costs, 55
  eligibility, 27–29
  system size and demographics, 29

Well-being, women, 45–46
Withdrawal, as birth control method, 15, 116, 200
Wolfers, Justin, 36, 38, 45–46
Women vs. men. See Men vs. women
Women's employment
  balancing career and children, 115
  birth control's effect on careers, 44, 94, 120
  sex drive questions, 96
  supporting families, 115, 117–118
  traditional nurturing roles, 40–41, 42, 88, 94
Women's happiness, 45–46, 176–177
Wood, Susan, 187
Woodling, John, 121
Woodsong, Cynthia, 43
Woolridge, Frosty, 53–58
World Health Organization, 54
World hunger, 54

Y

Youth. See Minors
Yuzpe, Albert, and Yuzpe regimen, 19–20, 65